NEBS MANAGEMENT DEVELOPMENT SUPER SERIES

THIRD EDITION

Managing Information

Communication in Management

Published for
&NEBS Management *by*

Pergamon
Flexible
Learning

Pergamon Flexible Learning
An imprint of Butterworth-Heinemann
Linacre House, Jordan Hill, Oxford OX2 8DP
225 Wildwood Avenue, Woburn, MA 01801-2041
A division of Reed Educational and Professional Publishing Ltd

A member of the Reed Elsevier plc group

OXFORD   AUCKLAND   BOSTON
JOHANNESBURG   MELBOURNE   NEW DELHI

First published 1986
Second edition 1991
Third edition 1997
Reprinted 1999 (twice), 2000

© NEBS Management 1986, 1991, 1996

All rights reserved. No part of this publication may be reproduced in any material form (including photocopying or storing in any medium by electronic means and whether or not transiently or incidentally to some other use of this publication) without the written permission of the copyright holder except in accordance with the provisions of the Copyright, Designs and Patents Act 1988 or under the terms of a licence issued by the Copyright Licensing Agency Ltd, 90 Tottenham Court Road, London, England W1P 0LP. Applications for the copyright holder's written permission to reproduce any part of this publication should be addressed to the publishers.

British Library Cataloguing in Publication Data
A catalogue record for this book is available from the British Library

ISBN 0 7506 3328 X

The views expressed in this work are those of the authors and do not necessarily reflect those of the National Examining Board for Supervision and Management or of the publisher.

NEBS Management Project Manager: Diana Thomas
Author: Pip Hardy
Editor: Diana Thomas
Series Editor: Diana Thomas
Based on previous material by: Jan Whitehead
Composition by Genesis Typesetting, Rochester, Kent
Printed and bound in Great Britain

Contents

Workbook introduction — v
1. NEBS Management Super Series 3 study links — v
2. S/NVQ links — vi
3. Workbook objectives — vi
4. Activity planner — vii

Session A The nature of communication — 1
1. Introduction — 1
2. The importance of good communication at work — 1
3. The basic skills — 3
4. The communication process: a model — 8
5. Communication feedback — 18
6. Planning communication — 22
7. **Summary** — 29

Session B The skills of communicating — 31
1. Introduction — 31
2. Communication systems — 31
3. Basic principles — 35
4. Methods of communicating — 36
5. Writing skills — 38
6. Speaking skills — 43
7. Body language, or non-verbal communication — 46
8. **Summary** — 53

Session C The skill of listening — 55
1. Introduction — 55
2. The importance of listening — 55
3. Barriers to effective listening — 56
4. Characteristics of good listeners — 58
5. Listening to behaviour — 62
6. **Summary** — 65

Performance checks — 67
1. Quick quiz — 67
2. Workbook assessment — 70
3. Work-based assignment — 71

Reflect and review — 73
1. Reflect and review — 73
2. Action plan — 75
3. Extensions — 77
4. Answers to self-assessment questions — 77
5. Answers to the quick quiz — 79
6. Certificate — 82

Workbook introduction

1 NEBS Management Super Series 3 study links

Here are the workbook titles in each module which link with *Communicaion in Management*, should you wish to extend your study to other Super Series workbooks. There is a brief description of each workbook in the User Guide.

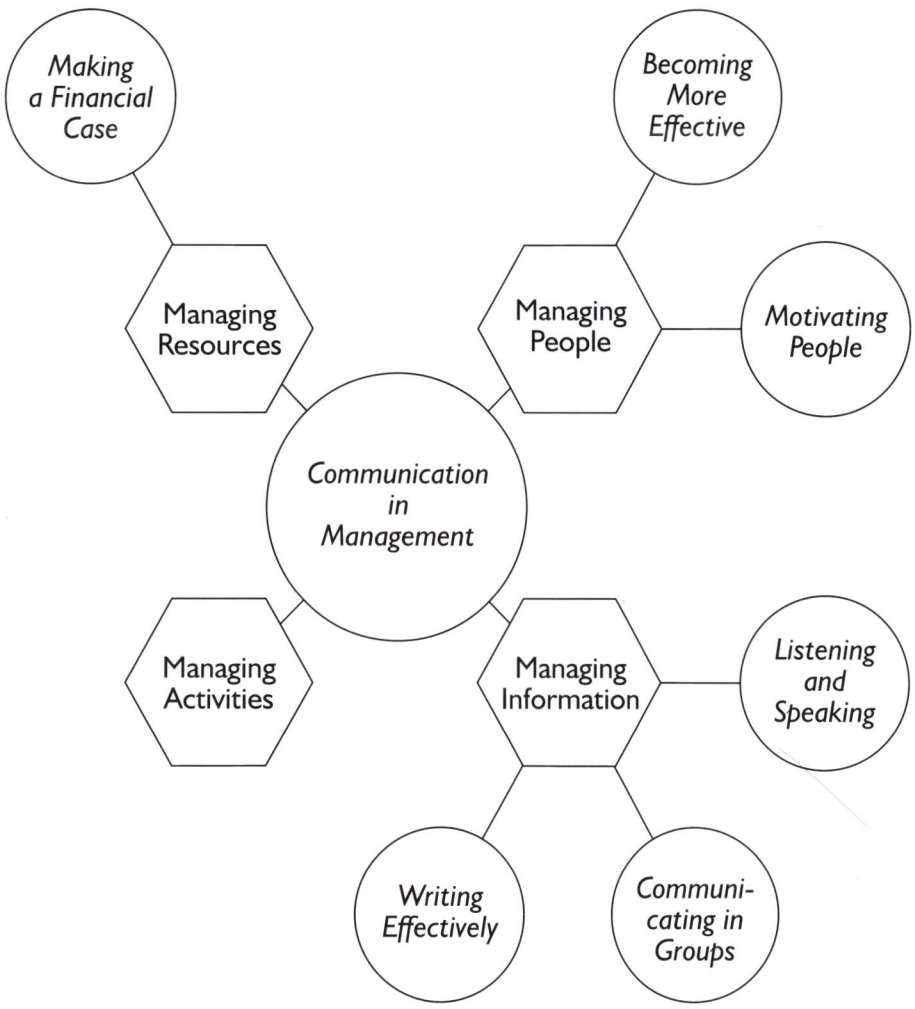

Workbook introduction

2 S/NVQ links

This workbook relates to the following elements:

C4.1   Gain the trust and support of colleagues and team members
D1.1   Gather required information
D1.2   Inform and advise others

It will also help you develop the following Personal Competences:

- relating to others;
- communicating.

3 Workbook objectives

'Communications' is one of the management buzz-words of the late twentieth century. Probably any manager you ask would agree that communications are very important but they would not all mean the same thing by that.

Some chief executives might pride themselves on having excellent communications in their organizations because they have a corporate video which is seen by a global workforce of thousands. Certainly such an initiative can bring strategic information to a lot of people who would otherwise not receive it. But is that what we really mean by 'communication'?

Other managers may see the importance of communication reflected in the fact that their organizations have the latest information technology so that everybody has at their fingertips the information they need, and the barriers of time and distance are largely overcome. In our working lifetime tremendous advances have been made in this aspect of communication and you probably feel that you have access to far more information than was possible two or three years ago. But is that all there is to communications? Does having the benefit of available technology mean that you and other managers in your organization are good communicators? Not necessarily.

It is still quite possible for an organization with the latest technological wizardry to be a communications disaster area. Why?

Because information is still seen as a source of power to be hoarded as a miser would gold? Because people are swamped with information whether they need it or not? Because people are not felt to matter that much and the time it would take to talk to them, still more to listen to them, is seen as a low management priority? Because although the means and the techniques for communication are there, the **will** to use them is lacking?

No matter what the technological advances or the current organizational theories the need for effective personal communication skills remains critical

Workbook introduction

to the success of every manager from the newly appointed team leader to the chief executive of a multinational company and it is these basic skills on which we will focus in this workbook.

We shall see that communication is only partly to do with passing on information. It is as much to do with listening and observing and modifying your behaviour in the light of what you see. Underpinning that, the way you communicate with people is indicative of the respect you have for them and the way you come across is what will earn you their respect in return.

The underlying purpose of communicating effectively is to create a reputation for being honest, approachable, competent and courteous. That is not earned simply by what you say but by your whole performance as a manager. When we talk about communications, therefore, there is a lot on the line about just how good a manager you really are.

3.1 Objectives

At the end of this workbook you should be better able to:

- identify the benefits to you of being a good communicator;
- design your communications to achieve the results you want;
- communicate more effectively in speech, writing and behaviour;
- listen effectively.

4 Activity planner

The following Activities need some planning and you may want to look at these now.

Most significantly, in this workbook we suggest that you ask someone to be a 'communications partner'. This is somebody, perhaps a member of your workteam or a colleague in a similar job to yours, who is familiar with your organization and who sees you in operation. Your communications partner would need to be willing to work through some of the activities with you and comment on how you communicate in your job. You will need to have a pretty good understanding with each other!

Activity 4 asks you to analyse the communications skills you use predominantly and to identify those which most affect the people you work with.

Activity 18 asks you to explore barriers to communication in your workplace and to identify ways in which they can be minimized. You will need to do this in relation to a specific situation over which you have or had some control. Involving a communications partner will give you more insight into what actually took place.

Workbook introduction

Activity 33 asks you to think about the effect of your body language. You need the comments of your communications partner rather than just your own perception and if a video camera or CCTV is available you will gain a much greater insight into the real message you convey as opposed to simply what you say.

Activity 39 suggests that you should arrange a listening session with your communications partner to explore how good your listening skills really are.

Portfolio of evidence

Some or all of these Activities may provide the basis of evidence for your S/NVQ portfolio. All Portfolio Activities and the Work-based assignment are signposted with this icon.

The icon states the elements to which the Portfolio Activities and Work-based assignment relate.

Session A The nature of communication

1 Introduction

Whether you manage the day-to-day work of other people in an office, leisure centre, bank, hotel, foundry or assembly shop, you will have one job characteristic in common with every other manager – you need to be able to communicate well to manage the activities of your work group. Communication is an essential supervisory skill.

> **EXTENSION 1**
> The vital role that communicating plays in the job of a front line manager is shown in the BBC Training Video series *Frontliners*. The way you communicate is a window on what you are.

We must communicate well to manage well – good communication is also the basis for good relationships.

In this part of the workbook we will start by defining the term 'communication' and deciding why it is so important to achieving our objectives as front line managers. Then we will think about the basic communication skills we all use. We will go on to look at a simple model of the communication process and at some of the ways of putting the model into practice. Finally, there are some basic principles for planning your communication.

2 The importance of good communication at work

Let's start by producing a working definition of this commonly used word 'communication'. It is only when we understand fully what communication involves that we can start thinking about improving our skills.

Activity 1

Think about the word 'communication' and what it means to you. Look up the word in a good dictionary, if you wish. Then jot down a sentence or two which describes fully what the word means.

Session A

Your definition of communication might be similar to these two below:

- 'saying something to somebody';
- 'making yourself understood'.

In a dictionary, you will find definitions similar to the following:

- 'the transfer of ideas between two people';
- 'the exchange of information';
- 'sharing information, making connections';
- 'the passing of instructions between people which results in action'.

These phrases make some valuable points about the nature of communication:

- it involves a sender and one or more receivers;
- a message is transferred or shared between two or more people;
- communication is also about community – it is only necessary when there is more than one person involved, but then it is essential for the smooth functioning of the group;
- it is a two-way process because the transfer of the message results in some kind of response.

You will find many descriptions to choose from, each one with its own merits. A good working definition which we will use in this unit is:

Communication is the transfer of information between people, usually resulting in action.

Communication is rightly regarded by employers as an essential part of a manager's job. Let's think about what happens when we fail to communicate.

Activity 2

If you failed to give instructions to your work group about how to carry out a task that was new to them, what do you think would be the result? Write down **two** outcomes that might result.

_____

_____

Here are some points you might have thought of.

- No one would carry out the task at all.
- The task would be done badly.
- Each individual would carry out the task in the way he or she thought was suitable.

Session A

You would not be able to achieve your own work group objectives and it would be harmful to your group's productivity and to their morale.

Communication may serve a wide range of work purposes. We need to communicate to:

- instruct;
- inform;
- persuade, encourage or suggest;
- consult or negotiate.

We communicate with management, members of our work group and other front line managers to ensure that our ideas and information are received, understood and acted upon by others.

Communication brings the minds and actions of people closer together to achieve objectives.

Now that we have decided why we communicate, let's move on to look at the skills we need.

3 The basic skills

In your daily management duties there are a number of skills you may use when communicating. These can be classified simply as follows.

- Speaking

  You communicate by talking to people face-to-face or on the telephone;

- Writing

  Communication in writing (whether on paper or screen) may involve writing letters, memos and reports;

- Behaving

  You communicate by what you actually do and how you look;

- Listening

  Listening to what others are saying is an essential part of the communication process.

You will probably find that you use a number of these skills together in the duties you undertake. The next Activity should help you to recognize the main communication skills involved in some typical supervisory activities.

Session A

Activity 3

Here are nine typical activities undertaken by front line managers. In each case tick the appropriate column for the main communication skills you would use when carrying out that duty.

Management Tasks	Speaking	Writing	Behaving	Listening
Establishing a good working relationship				
Giving instructions to workteam members				
Reporting progress to management				
Receiving suggestions from your work group for ways of improving work methods				
Filling in forms and work logs				
Maintaining fair discipline				
Meeting with other colleagues, customers or suppliers				
Giving training to new staff				
Dealing with problems and grievances				

You will find our suggestions below with a brief explanation. Your choices may have been slightly different. Differences are not too important at this stage as the main purpose of the Activity was to encourage you to think about the communication skills you actually use for specific duties and to show that you use the full range of skills within your own job.

Session A

- **Establishing good working relationships with team members**

    You will almost certainly need to use all the skills for this, but behaviour may be the most important. Your team will take their cue from the way you act and respond to situations.

- **Giving instructions to workteam members**

    Speaking and listening – you will have to tell them what you want, but it is just as important to listen to their responses which will help you to determine whether they have understood.

- **Reporting progress to management**

    Writing provides a permanent record and may help you to organize your thoughts. There may be many occasions when oral reporting (speaking) would be appropriate.

- **Receiving suggestions from your work group**

    Listening followed by behaving – you need to demonstrate that you are willing to consider their views and you need to act on some of their suggestions if you want them to keep contributing.

- **Filling in forms and work logs**

    Writing – there is no other way of carrying out this duty!

- **Maintaining fair discipline**

    Behaving – setting a good example is the best way to show that you are fair.

- **Meeting with other colleagues, customers and suppliers**

    Speaking and listening – it is just as important to listen to what others have to say as to make your own points.

- **Giving training to new staff**

    Speaking, behaving and listening – training usually involves explanation and demonstration. You also need to listen for questions and misunderstandings so that these can be put right as soon as possible. In some cases written reference material may need to be provided as well.

- **Dealing with problems and grievances**

    Listening followed by behaving – you need to fully understand the nature of the problem and it would probably require some action on your part to resolve it.

Session A

 **Activity 4**

Portfolio of evidence C5.1, D1.1, D1.2

15 mins

This Activity may provide the basis of appropriate evidence for your S/NVQ portfolio. If you are intending to take this course of action, it might be better to write your answers on separate sheets of paper.

Here is the list of typical front line manager activities again. Think about your own job and add to or delete from that list so that it reflects the major activities of your job. Now for each Activity enter a rough percentage for each communication skill. This means that if you read across all columns horizontally, each line should total 100%. This is where it is useful to get the opinion of someone who **sees** you communicating. What you do in practice may be rather different from how you see yourself.

Management Tasks	Speaking	Writing	Behaving	Listening
Establishing a good working relationship				
Giving instructions to workteam members				
Reporting progress to management				
Receiving suggestions from your work group for ways of improving work methods				
Filling in forms and work logs				
Maintaining fair discipline				
Meeting with other colleagues, customers or suppliers				
Giving training to new staff				
Dealing with problems and grievances				
Total				

Session A

Perhaps you were able to see at a glance that the main thrust of your communication relies on one particular skill. If it is not immediately obvious it may be enlightening to add up the columns vertically and see if one skill seems to predominate overall.

Managers are frequently surprised by the proportion of their time they spend (or should spend) listening, and are often made aware by team members or colleagues of the extent of the effect of their behaviour in their overall communication.

If you find a particular communication activity challenging or difficult (many people find making a formal presentation daunting, for example) it may become disproportionately significant when you think about your performance as a communicator. Quite possibly you spend much more of your time on the telephone or walking the job and talking to and listening to your workteam. In terms of your overall performance as a manager it is skills in these activities which will contribute more to your effectiveness.

Portfolio of evidence D1.1 — Activity 5

This Activity may provide the basis of appropriate evidence for your S/NVQ portfolio. If you are intending to take this course of action, it might be better to write your answers on separate sheets of paper.

Following the analysis you did in Activity 4, identify the communication skills you particularly need to improve. You should start to think how you might set about this as you study the rest of this workbook and could pull your plans together in the Action plan at the end of the workbook.

_____
_____
_____
_____
_____
_____

Whatever skills you are using, there is a basic process involved in all communication. We will look at this process next.

7

Session A

4 The communication process: a model

Our earlier definition of communicating was 'the transfer of information between people, resulting in action', so it has these main elements.

- People

    People are involved both as senders and as receivers of information.

- Information

    We communicate because we want to convey or receive information.

- Feedback

    The purpose of conveying most information is to achieve a specific result. The feedback may take the form of immediate action, but if it is not immediate, there must still be some way of acknowledging receipt and understanding of the information.

We can convert these three features into a simple model, which represents the communication process. It is important to remember the two-way nature of communication.

Activity 6

Thinking about the nature of communication as well as your own experience, try to draw a simple diagram or picture to show what happens when communication takes place.

Session A

There are many possibilities for the kind of model you might have drawn. Here are a few of them. The important thing is that your version indicate that good communication **always** involves two or more people. Communication models are often circlular to stress the on-going nature of communication.

Session A

Here is our diagrammatic communication model: we will use this as the basis for the rest of the workbook.

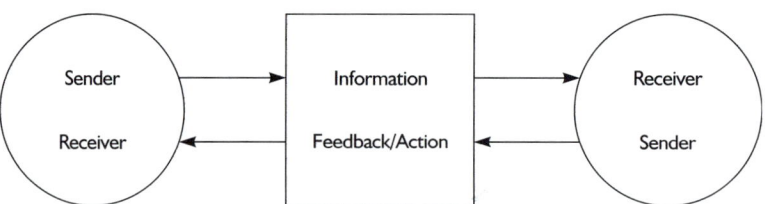

One person, the sender, sends information to another person, the receiver. The receiver will acknowledge in some way that the communication has been received and understood. If the communication is successful, in other words, the receiver understands the information correctly, some kind of action will probably be the result.

4.1 Information

> A lot of information where it is **not** needed is **not** communication.

Information is the substance of communication and is sometimes referred to as the message. It is what we want to say. You always need to be very clear about the substance of any communication at the outset.

We can use the case in the following Activity to show the difference between the substance of communication (the message) and the way it is transmitted (sometimes called the medium or media).

Activity 7

■ Jane Mansell is the supervisor in a section which enters insurance information onto computer files. She walks into the office one morning and finds Timothy Powell, an operator, drinking coffee at his terminal despite company policy which does not allow drinks near terminals.

What is the substance of the information Jane needs to convey to Tim?

If you were in Jane's place, what words would you use to convey the information to Tim?

Session A

You'll probably agree that the substance of Jane's information is that drinks should not be drunk at terminals. However, there are many ways she could actually convey that message. Several ways are given below.

- A heavy-handed question – 'Why have you disobeyed me by drinking coffee at your terminal, Tim?'
- An order – 'Please take your coffee away from your terminal at once, Tim.'
- A statement – 'I see you've disobeyed my instructions by drinking your coffee at your terminal, Tim.'
- A concerned question – 'Is everything alright? You don't normally drink your coffee here . . .'
- A message in writing – Jane might say nothing, but instead send Tim a brief memo or put up a notice reminding people that they should not be drinking at their desks.

Depending on Jane's relationships with her team, she might use any of these methods – and she could expect different responses from each. It is as well to be aware of the possible responses from different people – most people do not appreciate being disciplined in public. Effective front line managers are sensitive to the feelings of their team members – Tim might have come into work early, or had some bad news that morning which might have explained (but not excused) his behaviour.

You may have your own variations of any of these. This second part of the Activity leads us into thinking about the next feature of the communication process: people.

4.2 People

Each time we communicate a message to someone else, we (the sender) determine how we will communicate with the other person (the receiver). We decide which words we will use, how we will phrase those words and the tone we will use.

Although the communication model is in itself simple, it is often people who make communication an extremely complex process. You will find that there are a number of factors that will affect your own choice of how you communicate. Your approach to communication will reflect:

- your own personality: you may be forthright or shy;
- your feelings at the time: you may be angry, resentful or happy;
- your attitude towards the people with whom you are communicating: you may like or distrust them;
- your knowledge: you may know very little or a great deal about what you are communicating;
- your experience: you may have previous experience of similar situations;
- the culture of the organization: there may be a traditional, formal and disciplined culture with clear role distinctions, or there may be a more relaxed one in which people are expected to speak up, express opinions and feelings regardless of their position in the organization.

Session A

So, your attitudes and your experiences, together with the culture, will determine how you send and receive information. These factors are sometimes referred to as the context, and could appear on our model surrounding the sender/receiver cycle. These same factors will also determine how you respond to information you receive from other people. The following example should help to explain this point.

- Charlene works in a large mail order office and is known to her teamleader as being work shy and always ready to complain about anything. Shami, on the other hand, is a high producer and always ready to co-operate over any work plan changes.

  The teamleader respects her colleagues and expects them to be responsible and to carry out the work as well as they can without being constantly policed. In return, she is very fair and real effort is recognized and rewarded.

  The teamleader has just set some work targets for the use of new equipment and asks Charlene how she is getting on with these targets. Her reply is, 'The target's too high. I may make it for the odd half-hour – there's no way anyone's going to keep up with those targets.'

  Shami's reply is, 'Well, I can't be sure yet, but I'm finding it difficult to stay up with the targets for more than half an hour. I think the others will be in the same boat.'

The substance of the message from Charlene and Shami is the same. However, the way the teamleader will interpret the message from each of them may be very different.

Most front line managers would use the past experience of Charlene and Shami, i.e. that one was 'work shy' and the other a 'high producer', to put greater trust in the accuracy of the message received from Shami.

We all allow our attitudes and experiences to influence the meaning we give to information. The culture will also have some effect on how we communicate: whether we issue orders, make polite requests, listen to (and act on) suggestions from team members.

In written communication, we often refer to it as 'reading between the lines'. The substance of the information is frequently the least potent part of the message. It is the context of the message – these other human factors surrounding the message – which are more powerful in determining the way it is interpreted.

Here's another Activity which demonstrates this point.

> How information is presented is more powerful than what is being said. You may have heard the saying 'The medium is the message' (Marshall McLuhan) which is another way of saying the same thing.

Session A

Activity 8

Think of yourself as a customer on the receiving end of the following communications.

- A sales assistant in a shop comes up to you slouching, with his head down and says 'Can I help you?' in a bored tone of voice.

    What message do you actually receive?

- You receive a promotional letter from a hotel chain stating the efficiency and caring attitude of their staff, but the letter is badly typed, contains spelling mistakes and is unsigned.

    What message do you actually receive?

Most people would receive a very different message from what is actually said or written. As a result, the sales assistant is unlikely to make a sale and the hotel is most unlikely to get your custom. So the communication has not resulted in the right action.

4.3 Feedback

Although the hotel and the shop assistant have both sent some information, they have no way of knowing whether they have communicated successfully unless you respond.

Session A

Activity 9

- What would have been your response to the bored shop assistant?
  _____
  _____
  _____

- And to the hotel chain's poorly produced letter?
  _____
  _____
  _____

You might actually have said 'No, thanks' to the shop assistant and gone somewhere else for your shopping. Or you might have persevered, and asked for what you wanted. Depending on his next reaction, you might have become angry and decided not to buy anything. However, unless you were able to say something about his attitude he might never know why he lost your business.

As for the hotel's letter. You are unlikely to respond positively. Few people take the time to reply to such letters informing the sender of their reaction. But this is the only way they will know the reasons why they are getting so little business. So feedback is important and may lead to action: in both of these cases, something might happen. The shop assistant might have been encouraged to improve his attitude while the hotel chain might actually apply better quality control methods to its marketing strategies.

4.4 Action

Most communication has a purpose: it should result in some kind of action. The word 'action' usually conjures up the image of some kind of physical activity which can be observed. Here is an example of what I mean.

- Information: 'Go to my office and bring me the file for the Bartons account.'
- People: supervisor to clerk.
- Action: clerk goes to the office and returns with the file.

Sometimes communication results in action which is difficult to observe. Try the following Activity.

Session A

Activity 10

- A supervisor sends a routine progress report to a manager stating an increase in output for the month from 250 units to 300 units.

What results might there be from this communication that it are impossible to see? Jot down **two** suggestions.

You might agree that this transfer of information could result in:

- adding to the manager's existing knowledge;
- confirming (or reversing) the manager's existing impression about trends;
- confirming (or reversing) the manager's attitudes towards the supervisor and the work group.

These results are producing changes in the manager's way of thinking rather than observed action. We have already seen that action usually means a change in behaviour but changes in the mind are actions too.

4.5 Barriers to communication

So far the model looks deceptively simple. There is a complication which needs to be considered: the existence of barriers to communication, which prevent the information from being interpreted properly by whoever is receiving it.

We have already covered one barrier to effective communication – the attitudes and experiences of the receiver. If hostile attitudes exist and there have been poor relationships between sender and receiver arising from previous encounters, any new communication runs the risk of being misinterpreted or ignored.

Session A

Activity 11

Can you think of other barriers that you have encountered which have hindered the actual transmission of information to the receiver? Try to think of at least **three**.

_____
_____
_____
_____
_____
_____

Once you started on this Activity you probably thought of more than three. Here are some possible barriers, categorized under headings.

- Noise

Any kind of noise, whether it is machinery, printers, telephones, traffic or people, can make it difficult to hear or concentrate and may cause distortion of a message.

- Language

Sometimes the words that are used in communication cause the message to be misinterpreted. This can happen if imprecise words are used, for example 'sort of' or 'things'. Also, technical jargon can be confusing if it is unfamiliar to the other person. For instance, 'All you need to do is buy a 28,000 bps modem and get hooked up to an ISDN line and you'll be able to transfer files in the blink of an eye!'

- Environment

It is possible for people not to receive information properly because aspects of the work environment intervene, such as answering the telephone when someone is by your side trying to hold a conversation at the same time.

- Feelings

As we all know, feelings are very powerful. They can prevent us from hearing properly or may cause us to misunderstand information. How we feel about the person sending the information may cause us to distort the message; think how you would feel in Tim's situation, when he was reprimanded for drinking coffee at his terminal. Although some people are more sensitive than others, this conversation may affect his later communications with Jane. Or, if you are feeling upset, depressed or resentful, you may simply not take in information.

Session A

- Authority relationships

    Another barrier to effective communication you may have encountered is the pattern of authority relationships in organizations. Sometimes you may feel that communication has to go through some overcomplicated system to reach the right person and that, by the time it reaches them, it has become distorted. This leads to the next possible barrier.

- Culture

    We mentioned culture with respect to the way information is conveyed. It is a key factor in communication and can help or hinder communication. Imagine that you have been working in a very relaxed, small organization, where everyone takes responsibility for their own work and friendly relationships are the norm. Information is shared informally, with discussions taking place in order to ensure that messages have been understood. Then you take a new job in a larger organization with a strong hierarchical structure. Communication is quite formal, with lots of memos, formal meetings and rules and instructions. You may have become so used to the old way of communicating that it will be difficult to write memos, look for instructions, heed reprimands. Equally, someone coming from the larger organization to the smaller one might feel lost and somewhat out of control in the informal yet efficient culture there.

    So these barriers to communication exist for all of us. We cannot always remove them but we can recognize the effect they have and do our best to reduce their impact.

Activity 12

What could you do to reduce the barriers in the following situations?

- You sometimes do not hear messages correctly because you are distracted by the noise from printers and telephones in the open-plan office in which you work.

    _____

    _____

- You are often short-staffed because any request for new staff to fill vacancies is passed up to the departmental head (three levels above you) before it is passed on to Personnel.

    _____

    _____

Session A

Here are two alternatives for dealing with the first situation.

- You could investigate what could be done to reduce the noise from the printers and telephones, such as sound-proofing hoods on printers or using light signals rather than ringing tones for telephones.

- You could try to create a quiet work area by the use of partitioning/sound-proof screens.

The second situation is more difficult to resolve.

- You might be tempted to by-pass the formal system and go straight to Personnel but that would be undermining your management's authority – not a good move!

- You could discuss the matter with your manager, explain the problem and find out whether there is a valid reason for having authorization at top departmental level.

These barriers can hinder the transmission of information. However, in order for the communication process to be complete we must be sure that the receiver fully understands the message and will respond in a positive way. Let's look in more detail at the feedback part of the communication model.

5 Communication feedback

'One basic mistake, endlessly repeated, is to assume that what is known to us is known to everyone else.'

C. Northcote Parkinson and Nigel Rowe (1979), *Communicate*, Pan.

Often we think we have completed the communication process when we have given the other person the information. This means that we are assuming that it will lead to action. We can see the problems that arise from making these assumptions in the next Activity.

Session A

Activity 13

■ Atmoprint is a successful firm in the printing industry. They currently have more orders than they can easily cope with. An important rush printing order has just come in. Costas, the supervisor, decides to give this job to Margaret. He takes Margaret to the print room and explains how to operate the machine. He then gives Margaret the details of the order and leaves her to get on with it.

One hour later he realizes Margaret is still in the print room when she should have finished much earlier. Rushing down, Costas discovers that the order is not even half-completed and that Margaret is sitting unhappily at the machine, which is not running.

■ Did Costas follow the communication model we outlined earlier?

■ What could Costas have done which would have helped to avoid this problem? Try to think of **two** ways of avoiding this problem.

You may have decided that Costas could avoid this problem by:

- asking Margaret whether she understood;
- telling Margaret where he could be found and to come and find him as soon as she encountered any problems;
- staying to watch Margaret, to make sure Margaret was confident in operating the machine.

Costas did not actually follow our model in which communication only takes place when information has been sent, received, understood with some kind of feedback, possibly in the form of action. In fact, Costas neglected to ask himself two crucial questions which are important in all our communications:

- How do we know the other person understands the information?
- How can we be confident that the right action will result?

If we want to communicate effectively, we cannot leave the answers to these questions to chance. We must obtain some kind of message back from the receiver that our information has been fully understood. This feedback will reassure us that our communication has been successful.

Session A

You remember that we said earlier that we can identify two kinds of feedback from receivers. These are:

- feedback by action;
- feedback from the person.

If Costas gets Margaret to demonstrate that she can operate the machine by showing him, then the feedback comes from the action and can be incorporated into the model in the following way.

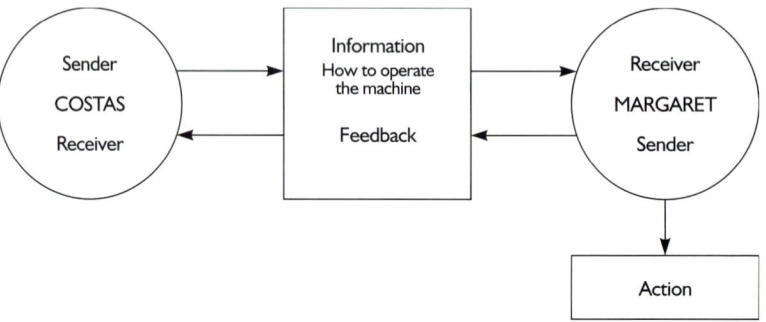

However, if Costas asks Margaret a question about whether she understands, then this is securing feedback from the person and can be shown like this:

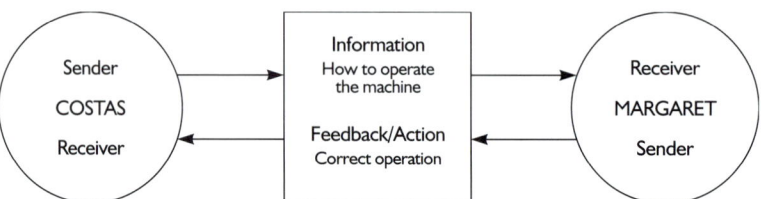

You have probably realized that action feedback is the better way of making sure that communication has been effective. Feedback from the person may cause more problems because a person will probably respond positively to the question which is asked even though they still may not understand. In this model the communication cycle is not complete because Costas still does not really know whether or not his instructions have been understood.

Let's go back to our case example in Activity 13.

Session A

Activity 14

- When Costas had finished his explanation of how the machine worked, he could have asked Margaret, 'Do you follow me? Are you clear about what you've got to do?'

Jot down why you think this might be a poor way of obtaining feedback.

Did you recognize that both these questions only allow for a yes or no answer? You are merely getting a statement of what the other person thinks she knows. If you ask these kinds of questions, there may be very good reasons why the receiver gives an inaccurate answer. For example, Margaret may answer 'Yes' to the questions merely because she does not want to appear slow, unintelligent, or incapable in front of her supervisor.

You may have experienced this yourself. Often people prefer to go away and fathom out a difficulty for themselves or to ask someone else after you have gone away. At the best, this wastes time and at the worst it may risk injury, spoilt materials or damaged equipment.

It is far better to ask a question that requires the other person to 'replay' the instruction. Here are some examples that Costas could have used.

- 'What do you think are the most important points to bear in mind when operating this machine?'
- 'We've looked at how this machine works and you've had a practice. Now, how are you going to tackle this order?'

You can also confirm a person's answers by looking at them and observing the way they behave. Look at their facial expressions and their gestures. Do they look confident and certain or do doubtful expressions cross their faces? Are they nodding or shaking their heads? Are they calm and controlled in their gestures and movement or are they nervous, jumpy and clumsy? You need to ask questions, listen to their replies and look at their reactions to see if they have fully understood and that understanding is likely to lead to action.

You can use these techniques to secure feedback in face-to-face situations but it may be more difficult to secure feedback from people or action when you are using written communication methods. In the next Activity you need to think about how you can obtain feedback when you are writing to people.

Session A

Activity 15

When you write a memo or a letter, how can you check whether the receivers have understood and are going to act in the way you want? Write down **two** ways you might achieve this.

_____

_____

_____

_____

Written communication is sometimes referred to as one-way communication because feedback may be delayed or even non-existent but it can be done. You can for instance:

- ask specific questions so that they have to write or telephone in order to answer the questions;
- state clearly the kind of response you want, for example, you can write, 'Please confirm this appointment by telephone before 12th June' rather than, 'I look forward to hearing from you as soon as possible';
- use the last sentence for stating the action you want, this means that it is the last information they read and therefore they should remember it more easily.

Getting feedback is important but may not always be easy. However:

Feedback helps to ensure that communication produces the required result.

6 Planning communication

As in all activities, half the success of effective communication comes from planning.

The more thought and effort we put into thinking through our communication in advance, the more likely it is to be successful. The immediate reply that most of us make when challenged about poor communication is, 'I'd communicate more effectively if I had the time to sit back, think and plan – but when does a busy supervisor find time to do this?'

Session A

Activity 16

Write down **three** of the factors that would influence the amount of time you spend on planning your communications, for example, the importance of the task.

_____

_____

_____

_____

You will probably agree that some of the most important factors are:

- your own knowledge and experience;
- the other person's knowledge and experience;
- the seriousness of failing to communicate effectively;
- how well you know and get on with the other person;
- the complexity of the information that needed to be communicated.

You will have to decide how much time you spend on planning each communication, but, whatever time you decide, there are some simple principles to follow in planning any communication. These are to be decided in advance and are listed below.

- **Why** you are communicating

    You need to be clear in your own mind about your purpose.

- **What** you are communicating

    You need to be clear about the substance of the information.

- **With whom** you are communicating

    You need to think what you know about the receiver including their knowledge, experience, skills, attitudes and previous relationship to you.

- **How** you should communicate

    You need to decide the most appropriate method of communicating and the way you will present the information.

In some cases you also need to decide the following:

- **When** you should communicate

    You should decide the best time for giving the information.

- **Where** you should communicate

    Sometimes the substance of the communication may require privacy and quiet or it may be better to discuss a matter off work premises.

Session A

Here is an example to illustrate these points.

- Robbie Dent was a supervisor in a firm manufacturing haulage gear to the mining industry. It was winter and a couple of the staff in Robbie's section were off with 'flu. Robbie noticed a patch of oil across a gangway. As there weren't many workers in and the tank section on the gangway wasn't staffed that morning, it wasn't an immediate problem but it was a safety hazard and needed to be cleaned up.

  He called across to Dougie, a newcomer to the section, who was bent over some work on his bench. 'There's some oil across the gangway up there, Dougie.'

  Dougie looked up briefly. 'Aye, could be nasty, that,' he agreed.

  'That's right,' Robbie said. 'It'll have to be cleaned up.'

  Just then, Robbie was called over to the offices to sort out order forms. While he was there he received a message that there had been an accident in his section. It was nothing serious, but someone who had arrived late had slipped and sprained his wrist. He'd be off work for a week.

  Robbie was furious. The accident had been caused by the oil patch. He went over to Dougie.

  'I told you to clean it up!' he said angrily.

  'No you didn't!' Dougie replied. 'If you had, I'd have done it.'

You can see that the information Robbie thought he'd given was not the information Dougie thought he heard. Let's explore the reasons behind this communication failure by returning to our basic communication model.

- People – Robbie (the sender) is treating Dougie (the receiver) as an 'old hand' and forgetting he is a newcomer.
- Information – the message is not clear. Is Robbie giving an instruction or is he merely passing on information as a warning? Is it clear what he wants to achieve?
- Action – Robbie does not convey in the information that the required action is for Dougie to clean up the oil.

Possibly the worst failure is the following:

- Feedback – Robbie does not use any technique to make sure that Dougie has understood his instruction correctly or set any specific time limits for carrying out the action.

Session A

Activity 17

Try using the four-point planning model of **why, what, who** and **how** to ensure that Robbie's communication is effective.

- Why does Robbie need to communicate?

  _____

- What is Robbie communicating?

  _____

- With whom is Robbie communicating? What do you know about Dougie?

  _____

- How should Robbie communicate to ensure that Dougie understands the information and takes the appropriate action?

  _____

  _____

Here is one possible response to that Activity:

- **Why:** Robbie needs to give an instruction to have the oil cleaned up so as to ensure a safe working environment.

- **What:** The information that needs to be conveyed is:
  - the danger of the oil
  - the need to have it cleaned up
  - the urgency with which this action should be taken.

- **Who:** Robbie needs to remember that Dougie is a newcomer and should not assume knowledge that Dougie may not possess.

- **How:** Robbie could call Dougie over to the patch of oil in order to focus his attention on the matter. He should ask him a question about the cleaning to make sure that Dougie has understood the instruction and knows where to get the cleaning materials. He should set a deadline for the action so that Dougie appreciates that action should be taken quickly.

Communication planning does not need to be a lengthy process each time. However, conscious decisions about why, what, who and how do need to be made. Remember: a moment's planning can prove to be very worthwhile in achieving results.

Session A

 **Activity 18**

Portfolio of evidence C4.1, D1.1, D1.2

20 mins

This Activity may provide the basis of appropriate evidence for your S/NVQ portfolio. If you are intending to take this course of action, it might be better to write your answers on separate sheets of paper.

Identify one important communication activity which you regularly carry out and which affects your workteam. (Choose something which is important to the operation of the workteam or to individual team members such as giving instructions on how a job is to be done or coaching a new team member rather than something which is necessarily challenging to you.) Look back at your analysis of your communication role in Activity 4 if you need a prompt.

Make a note of who is the receiver in the situation you have in mind and what is the real purpose of the message. Now think about how you carry out your chosen activity from the team member's point of view and identify any barriers to communication which you think the receiver experiences. You would benefit from asking your communication partner's reaction to this. Make a note of things you can do to remove the barriers to communication.

Receiver _____

Message _____

Purpose _____

How do you communicate?

_____

_____

Barriers to communication	Action to improve communication

26

Session A

That last Activity may have prompted you to have a serious re-think about a continuing failure to get your message across or you may have focused on something which, when you have the time to stop and think about it, is obvious and simple to put right, such as giving instructions indoors before going on a noisy site or coaching a new trainee out of earshot of the rest of the team so that he or she feels less conspicuous. Hopefully it has delivered a practical result.

Activity 19

Portfolio of evidence C4.1, D1.1, D1.2

10 mins

This Activity may provide the basis of appropriate evidence for your S/NVQ portfolio. If you are intending to take this course of action, it might be better to write your answers on separate sheets of paper.

Go back to the situation you considered in Activity 18. This time, list the feedback you currently expect from the communication exchange you are exploring. Is it people feedback or action feedback?

What would be the practical benefits of ensuring that you get action feedback?

Make a note of ways in which you could get action feedback. What use will you make of the feedback you obtain?

Once again, this Activity may be the stimulus for a radical change in your work practice or it may result in a minor improvement such as detecting a misunderstanding before any time or resources have been wasted.

Getting action feedback should become a way of life and can avoid a great deal of waste and frustration all round.

27

Session A

Self-assessment 1

1 Complete the following sentences with the suitable word or words chosen from the following list.

FEEDBACK	WHO	FEELINGS
INFORMATION	ATTITUDES	PEOPLE
HOW	LANGUAGE	PLANNED
CULTURE	ACTION	EXPERIENCE
MIND		

a The communication model has three key features; these are _____, people and _____.

b Feedback can come from action and from _____.

c Action can involve a change of _____ as well as a change of behaviour.

d Our four-point planning model for communication asks what, why, _____ and _____.

e Some barriers to communication include _____, _____, _____ and environment.

f _____ is essential to the communication process.

g Our _____ and _____ affect the way we communicate.

h All communication needs to be _____.

2 How can you make sure that someone has understood a written communication they have received from you?

_____

_____

_____

3 List **three** things which will influence the amount of time you spend planning communications.

_____

_____

_____

Answers to these questions can be found on pages 77–8.

Session A

7 Summary

- The purpose of communication is:
    - to bring the minds and actions of people closer together
    - to share information.

- The basic skills of communicating are:
    - speaking;
    - writing;
    - behaving;
    - listening.

- A model of the communication process is:

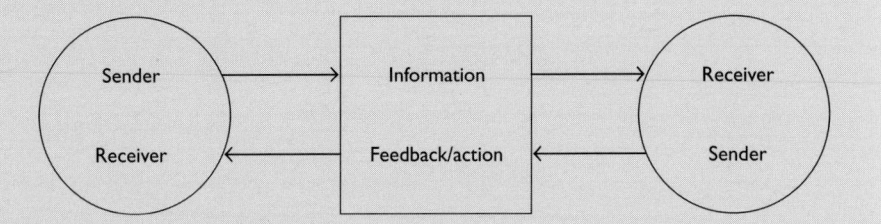

```
  ┌────────┐      ┌─────────────┐      ┌────────┐
  │ Sender │ ───▶ │ Information │ ───▶ │Receiver│
  │Receiver│ ◀─── │Feedback/    │ ◀─── │ Sender │
  └────────┘      │   action    │      └────────┘
                  └─────────────┘
```

  in which:

    - information is the substance of the communication;
    - people act as senders and receivers and are affected by past experiences and attitudes (context) and culture;
    - action is what we do and also what we think.

- Feedback comes from two sources:
    - from the action itself – action feedback
    - from the person – person feedback.

- Communication planning involves thinking in advance about the following:
    - Why? Why do I need to communicate?
    - What? What do I want to say?
    - Who? With whom am I communicating?
    - How? How do I convey the message to ensure action?

Session B The skills of communicating

1 Introduction

Now that we have explored the nature of communication and why it is necessary to communicate, we'll move on to think about how communication happens and then develop some basic skills. First of all we will look at the kinds of communication systems that exist in organizations, as these will form the background for all your communication. Then we will look at the main skills you need to communicate: writing and speaking (listening is covered in Session C). We will consider some general principles and then we will examine the skills of writing and speaking in more detail. We will finish by examining communication through the way we look and behave.

2 Communication systems

Organizations have different structures and different cultures. You know that some organizations have a rigid hierarchy while others may be more relaxed and informal. These will determine the kinds of systems which are used for communication. Let's look at how communication works in organizations.

Here are the three main ways in which communication flows:

- Downwards communication, which flows from management to staff, instructs workers, explains job rationales, provides performance feedback and tells new employees what is expected of them.
- Upwards communication, from staff to management, provides feedback to managers and supervisors concerning how employees feel about their work, their responses and reactions to whatever is communicated downwards. It is also the main way of informing management about problems and changes required.
- Horizontal communication, between peers, is used to co-ordinate tasks, share information, solve problems and provide support to workmates.

Session B

Activity 20

5 mins

Read through the first part of the following case study and think about how this kind of structure might affect communication in the organization.

■ In one NHS Trust, managers and staff were appointed at 'levels of work'. The levels start at Level 1, for porters and health care assistants, and go up to Level 6 for the Chief Executive.

This strict hierarchy of levels has many implications for organizational communication. What do you think these might be?

■ This is what happened when the Trust was first set up:

Cliques often formed, where Level 4 managers might choose only to communicate with other Level 4s.

It can be difficult for people at lower levels to communicate with someone at a higher level and working in a different area. The message has to go all the way up from the Level 1 person via his or her own line, then travel sideways to the Level 4 that the person wishes to communicate with. The Level 4's response travels back sideways to the Level 4 at the top of the Level 1's line, and then all the way down to the person at Level 1. This increases the chances for information to be distorted and misunderstood as it passes up and down and across the hierarchy.

The levels are also used to target audiences for information and communication from Senior Management. A memo might be marked 'Brief to Level 4'. This should mean that no one at Levels 1, 2 or 3 is passed this information. Occasionally, however, a manager fails to notice the level to which the message should be briefed, and tells everyone. This causes problems because some people at Levels 1, 2 and 3 have been passed the information, but no others in the organization have received it. This can cause wild rumours to start flying and general discontent among all the people at Levels 1, 2 and 3.

You can see that this kind of structure could make it very difficult to communicate effectively.

Session B

Activity 21

Portfolio of evidence D1.1

20 mins

This Activity may provide the basis of appropriate evidence for your S/NVQ portfolio. If you are intending to take this course of action, it might be better to write your answers on separate sheets of paper.

Different models or systems for communication are appropriate for different kinds of organizational structure and different needs. Look at the diagrams below[1] and read the description of each. Then decide which is closest to the way communication happens where you work.

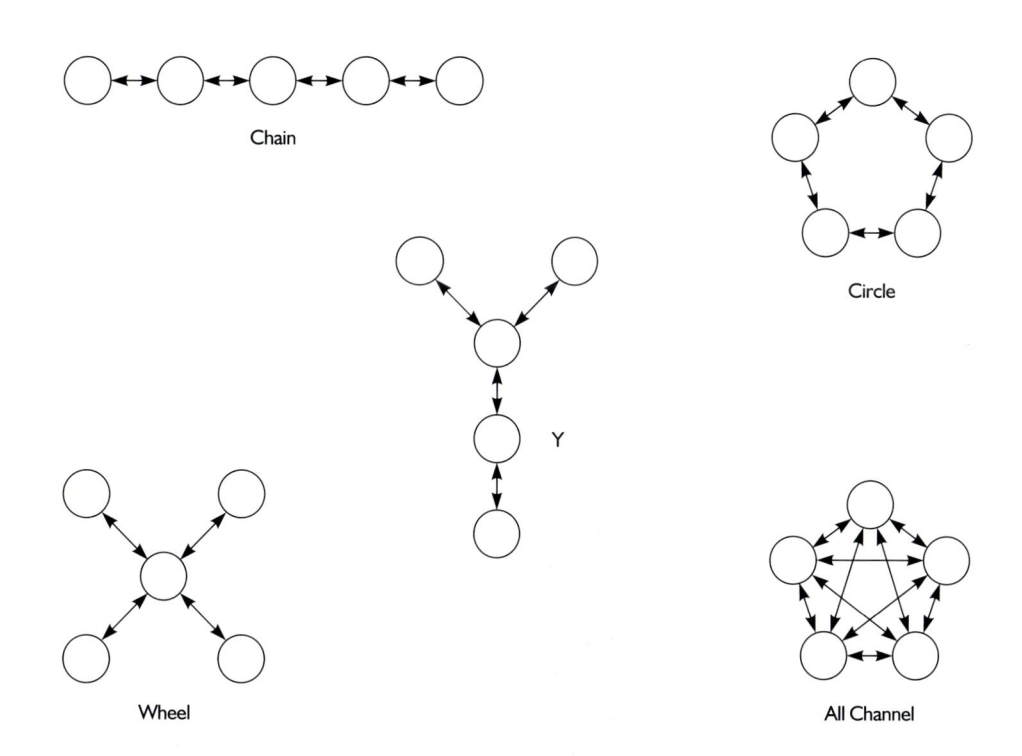

Chain

Y

Wheel

Circle

All Channel

- In the **chain** formation, each person communicates only with the people next to him or her in the chain. The people at each end of the chain communicates with only one other person.
- The **circle** formation is similar, but the end and the beginning of the chain are joined to form a circle. Each person communicates with two other people.
- The **Y** formation is like a chain that has split. The people at the top of the Y communicate only with the person who links them to the tail of the Y, which is like the chain formation.
- In the **wheel** formation, one person communicates with all the other people, each of whom communicates only with that central person.
- In the **all-channel** formation, each member of the group communicates with every other member of the group.

---

[1] Adapted from: Leavitt, H.J. (1951) 'Some effects of certain communication patterns on group performance.' *Journal of Abnormal and Social Psychology*, 46: 38–50.

Session B

The communication model which is closest to my own experience is _____.

Do you think this is the most appropriate one? If not, which model would be better? Why?

_____
_____

Is there anything you can do to change the communications model in your work area? This is something you may like to discuss with your communications partner.

_____
_____
_____
_____

Which model you choose depends on the situation. Where there is no need for confidentiality or secrecy, the best model may be where everyone can speak to everyone else as in the 'All Channel'. This is also the most satisfying in terms of relationships between group members.

Where information cannot be given out so freely, the most efficient communication structures seem to be those in which information goes through a central source, as in the Wheel or the Y. The systems which restrict communication, as in the Y, the Circle or the Chain, are the least efficient in co-operative tasks.

It's a good idea to be aware of the kind of structures and systems which operate as they affect your relationships with others as well as the way in which you choose to communicate.

Now let's look at some of the skills you need to send information.

Session B

3 Basic principles

We often find it easier when developing skills to have a few simple principles we can apply. This is true of communication skills. There are a couple of ways of helping to remember key principles of writing or speaking.

The first method is known as the ABC of communication. This stands for:

- **A**ccuracy

Information used at work must be accurate. For example, it's no good asking a customer to pick up goods at 4.00pm if they will not be ready until 5.00pm.

- **B**revity

People want relevant, essential information – not a lot of irrelevant, time-consuming extras.

- **C**larity

The message must be clear. If it is vague or can be interpreted in two or three different ways, it will not produce the correct action. An example of a vague, ambiguous message is: 'I think that order for Spratts is needed by lunchtime Thursday.'

> Too much communication is as harmful as too little. Tell people what they need to know but don't always swamp them with information and exhortation.
> C. Northcote Parkinson and Nigel Rowe (1979), *Communicate*, Pan.

Activity 22
8 mins

Look at the example we've just given about the order for Spratts. Work out why it's vague and ambiguous and then rewrite it so that the information is clear.

_____

_____

You could write it many ways but I hope you will agree that the following version eliminates all doubt.

The order for Spratts will be completed and ready for delivery by 12.00 noon on Thursday 8 February 199X.

Session B

Another way of remembering the characteristics of good communication skills is to think of the five C's of communication. These are that any communication should be:

- Clear

    The message must be clear so that there is only one possible meaning.

- Complete

    When you are writing or speaking you must include all the information that is needed to enable the appropriate action to be taken. We can often provide incomplete messages by omitting important points such as dates, times, names or amounts. Incomplete messages left on answering machines are good examples of how failure to observe this principle can frustrate receivers!

- Concise

    This means more than being brief. If you are so brief that you do not convey all the information needed, this is not good communication. Concise means brief but including all the relevant information.

- Correct

    It is essential that the information given is correct.

- Courteous

    Since you want some positive action to result from your communication, it is important that you maintain common courtesy and show respect for another person, whatever their level of authority may be within the organization. Most people do not respond well to an instruction which starts 'Hey, you over there …'. Generally the principle is – treat other people the way you would like to be treated!

Now let's think about these principles in relation to writing and speaking skills.

4 Methods of communicating

Before looking at specific skills, we'll pause for a minute to compare the advantages of written and spoken communication.

On many occasions within your working week you may be faced with a choice.

- Should I telephone a customer or write?
- Should I send a message by memo or e-mail or go and talk to the person?

Part of the success of communication depends on selecting the right method to meet the needs of the situation. We have given an example in the Activity below.

Session B

Activity 23

5 mins

- Indy is the senior ledger clerk in a large accounts department. One Monday morning, a departmental manager wanted some detailed sales figures for a meeting the following week. Indy decided to dictate these figures to him over the telephone.

Do you think this method of communicating was appropriate? Write down a reason for your decision.

_____
_____

You probably decided that it was not an appropriate method for communicating because:

- complex figures can be easily misheard over the telephone;
- unless she asks him to read the figures back, Indy has no feedback as to whether he noted them down correctly;
- there is no great urgency for the figures – the meeting is not until the following week. A printed set of figures would not necessarily be more accurate but would be less likely to be changed in transmission. Fax transmission would be as quick as a telephone call anyway.

Both written and spoken methods have their own advantages. You can use your own experience to identify some of these.

Activity 24

8 mins

Write down **two** situations in which it has been better to use written communication and **two** situations in which it has been better to use spoken communication.

- Written communication:

_____
_____

- Spoken communication:

_____
_____

Session B

You may like to compare your list with mine. I have quoted general rather than specific situations but I expect our lists are similar.

Some of the situations in which written communication is better are:

- when you need a permanent record of the information for future reference;
- when the information is the subject of a contract or agreement or when you think there may be disagreement arising from the information;
- when you want the receiver to be able to control the time and place they receive the message;
- when the information is confidential.

Some of the situations in which spoken communication is better are:

- when you want immediate feedback;
- when it is necessary to have an exchange of information or ideas;
- when it is a good idea to be able to use tone or body language to support the substance of the message;
- when you think it would be wiser not to have a permanent record.

You will need to think carefully each time which method you should use and weigh up the relative advantages. When you are doing this, it is helpful to think about the following factors.

- Clarity – Which method enables the information to be conveyed clearly and accurately?
- Speed – How quickly must the other person receive the message and respond to it?
- Cost effectiveness – Which method will achieve the desired result at least cost?
- Attitude of receivers – Which method is likely to be most acceptable to the receivers so that they will provide positive feedback?

Now we have compared the two methods, let's move on to examine writing skills in more detail.

5 Writing skills

You will certainly find that a proportion of your time will be spent writing. You may even complain that your supervisory job involves too much pen-pushing! It is important that you develop writing skills which allow you to achieve the results you want as quickly and easily as possible. Your writing may involve:

- making entries on a variety of forms;
- passing on written messages from one shift to another;
- taking down telephone messages to pass on to your manager or to a member of your workteam;
- making out accident reports or progress reports;

Session B

- sending memos or e-mail to other people within the organization;
- sending letters to customers, clients, suppliers and other people outside the organization.

Before we move into a more detailed exploration of writing skills, there is one important fact to bear in mind; that is, whenever you put pen to paper, you are making a statement about yourself and your organization. What you write and how you write it conveys an image of you to someone else.

> Every piece of writing projects an image of you.

Activity 25

8 mins

If you write letters to people outside your organization, what sort of impression do you think they get of you and your organization from your letters?

_____

Try to identify at least **three** points about your letters which convey this impression.

_____
_____
_____

The impression you may get of other companies from their letters can be that they are inefficient, indifferent and couldn't care less about the customer.

You can convey a good or a bad impression in a letter from:

- the way you set out the letter on the page – its layout;
- the sequence in which you present the information;
- the actual words you use;
- the accuracy of your use of English;
- the tone that is conveyed by the phrasing you use.

These points are also important in other forms of written communication you use inside your organization – memos, messages and reports. The success behind written communication is to keep your reader clearly in your mind when you prepare and write. You do not have the advantage of immediate feedback, as you do in face-to-face communication, so there are several things that you must anticipate.

Session B

- **Existing knowledge**

    You must decide what the readers already know about the subject.

- **Additional information required**

    You must decide what additional information your readers need or want to know.

- **Vocabulary range**

    You must consider the likely range of words used by your readers, including their understanding of technical terms.

- **Tone**

    You must choose your words and phrases very carefully so that other people understand the message and are willing to take the action you require. You do not want to create a negative reaction in your readers.

- **Sequence and layout**

    You want to present information in an order which is simple and easy for readers to follow. Likewise, the overall layout needs to attract readers to want to read the message.

Activity 26

6 mins

Look at the following two versions of a memo sent by Charles Read to Palminder Singh, a manager in another department to whom he has spoken once on the telephone. Decide which is the better memo and note down your reasons.

- **Version 1**

    From: Charles

    To: Palminder

    Thanks for the file and the info. I'll burn the midnight oil on this one and let you know the final figures tomorrow. OK?

Session B

■ **Version 2**

From: Charles Read Senior Bookkeeper

To: Palminder Singh Marketing Manager

Date: 25 September 1990

Parker file

Thanks for sending me the Parker file and the additional information. I'll be looking at the contents tonight and will calculate the final costings.

The final figures will be on your desk by 10.30am tomorrow. If you need them earlier than this, please ring me on extension 308 before 5.00pm today.

Version _____ is better because:

_____
_____
_____

You will probably agree that Version 2 is better. The two versions are contrasted in the explanation below.

■ Version 2 provides clear, complete and correct information.

Version 1	Version 2
Does not clearly identify the sender of the memo	Gives the sender's full name and job position
Does not state clearly which file has been received – Palminder could send out many files!	States the name of the file for clear identification
Omits important information from the memo headings, that is, the date and the subject	Gives a date in the memo headings so that there is a clear reference point for words such as 'today' and 'tomorrow'
	Also provides a subject heading so that there is instant recognition of the subject of the memo

Session B

- Version 2 considers the reader of the memo more carefully.

Version 1	Version 2
Uses the expression 'burning the midnight oil', which could confuse Palminder	Uses simple, everyday words
Is over-casual in tone for a supervisor to a manager who is virtually a stranger in another department.	Is more cautious and respectful of the manager's position and attitudes.

The first version runs the risk of Palminder Singh being confused about the message and angry or resentful at the tone. It certainly does not convey a good image of Charles Read.

Therefore, when writing: keep your reader in the forefront of your mind.

This will go some way to compensate for the absence of immediate personal feedback.

Generally, written communication does give you more time for planning what you want to say and how to say it. It also allows you to check over what you have written before sending it. However, once committed to paper and sent, it is a permanent record – so do make sure it fulfils the basic communication principles.

In trying to achieve a good writing style, it is very tempting to copy a style from someone else. Sometimes this results in long, complicated sentences and outmoded expression. Some common examples are: 'We are in receipt of your esteemed communication', 'Thanking you for favouring us with your order.' These are reminiscent of a Victorian clerk with a quill pen, so don't be tempted to use them. In other cases, written documents become a number of standardized expressions linked together in sentences – as though produced by an impersonal robot. Your employers may have certain standards they like maintained, but this should still allow you to devise a simple, straightforward style of writing which reflects your own personality.

> Devise your own style of writing.

We are very conscious of thinking about language and layout when we are writing. It is sometimes a different matter when we are speaking to people – which is what we'll look at next.

Session B

6 Speaking skills

The skills of speaking effectively are just as important as that of writing well.

The old saying 'Think before you speak' is a very true one.

Unfortunately it is something we often forget. We spend so much of our time each day talking to people face-to-face, formally or informally, that we forget that we need to give attention to developing our speaking skills if people are to understand us properly and act on our information.

If you think back to the basic communication model, you will appreciate that you need to be aware of the action you want to achieve before you start speaking.

Activity 27

6 mins

Think of a situation in the past when you have given spoken instructions and the resulting action was not what you wanted. Perhaps the task was done badly, was not done at all or was done unwillingly.

_____

Now jot down at least **three** examples of the way you gave the instructions, which contributed to the poor result.

_____
_____
_____

Here are a number of typical examples, perhaps your examples were similar.

- I didn't think clearly in advance about what I wanted to say and was therefore very vague.
- I didn't check that others were listening properly before I started.
- I used technical terms that people didn't fully understand.
- I used words and a way of speaking that could have been misinterpreted.
- I used a tone of voice that was too aggressive or too weak.
- I assumed people knew more than they did.
- I didn't ask questions to see if they had understood properly.

Session B

When things go wrong we often find excuses for ourselves. A typical comment we have probably all made at some time is, 'I know what I said but what I meant was ...'. Therefore, whenever you are talking to people face-to-face or on the telephone, you need to remember a few basic points.

- Prepare

    You need to be clear in your own mind what you want to say before you say it. This will help to make the message accurate and clear.

- Switch on the other person

    Make sure the other person is listening before you start. You can do this very simply by asking a question. Alternatively you can make a statement such as, 'I'd like to talk to you about ...'

- Speak clearly and audibly

    If you do, the listener won't have the embarrassment of having to ask you to repeat information.

- Use familiar words and phrases

    In this way there is less chance of being misunderstood. If new technical terms have to be used, make sure you explain them.

- Use a tone of voice which suits the situation

    The actual sound of your voice, combined with the words you choose, should convey the message accurately. For example, you would use a cheerful tone for good news, a cooler, more formal tone for a discipline interview.

- Playback

    Use questions to ensure that your listener can repeat the message accurately to you so you know that you have been understood correctly.

Finally, remember that people are more willing to respond positively, particularly to instructions, if they know **why** they have to do something. After all, can you do a really good job if you don't know why you're doing it? We will put some of the above points into practice in the next Activity.

Session B

Activity 28

5 mins

- A section supervisor in a bank is giving a new person who is about to start work as a clerk some last-minute instructions. She states: 'Finally, the bank demands that you look right.'

To what extent does this message fulfil the ABC of good communication?

- Accurate

- Brief

- Clear

I hope you gave that a resounding – 'Not very well!' For example:

- Accurate. Is it the bank or the supervisor who is making the demands? Is 'demands' the right word? Does this mean that disciplinary action can be taken?
- Brief. It is certainly brief – but at the expense of clarity. The message is incomplete. It does not provide sufficient detail.
- Clear. The message is totally unclear. The words 'look right' are far too vague. Does this apply to dress? If so, what dress code does the supervisor have in mind? Does it extend, for example, to hair styles?

Certainly this clerk will go away confused unless she asks some questions! She'll probably go and ask other clerks what the supervisor meant. Let's start again with this scenario from the supervisor's viewpoint.

- Preparation. The supervisor wants to convey the message that she likes female staff to wear simple, conservative clothes for work rather than high fashion and that hair should be clean and tidy.
- Switch on. She could ask a question about clothes or make a comment such as, 'That's a very smart suit you're wearing.'
- Speak clearly and audibly. It's always important to speak clearly, not to mumble or race through the words, and to look at people when talking to them. This is a way of showing respect.
- Use familiar words and phrases. She should use normal conversational vocabulary. If she uses technical terms such as 'dress code', she also needs to explain that this is a set of simple rules about the type of clothes people are expected to wear to work at the bank.

Session B

- Tone. The tone needs to be brisk, assertive but friendly. It should be brisk and assertive because she needs to convey that this is an essential part of the clerical job; friendly because she is advising a new employee, not reprimanding an existing member of the workteam for failing to obey the code.
- Playback. She can finish by saying, 'Now I've told you something about how we at the bank like clerks to look. Do you think there are likely to be any problems?' (She might have to take her cue from what the new clerk was actually wearing. If she was suitably dressed the supervisor could safely assume that she understands the code. If not, she might need to press a little harder to ensure the clerk understands the importance of the code.)
- Why. She should recognize that a new clerk would appreciate an explanation of why the dress code exists. The probable explanation is because clerks are visible to members of the public and the bank wants to convey a good public image of order and efficiency.

Now we have looked at some of the skills of speaking, let's turn to a set of skills which often accompany speaking in face-to-face situations, behaving skills.

7 Body language, or non-verbal communication

The third way in which we can communicate is by conveying a message through the way we look or behave – our body language. Very often we use behaviour to add weight to what we say. Try the following Activity.

Activity 29

5 mins

Write down three forms of behaviour you can use to reinforce the spoken message, 'No – I don't agree with that!'

_____

_____

_____

See if your list is similar to this one. You can:

- shake your head;
- glare at the other person;
- frown;
- cross your arms firmly;
- stamp your foot;
- bang your fist.

Session B

This example shows that we use the following aspects of body language to convey messages:

- eye contact;
- facial expressions;
- gestures;
- stance and posture.

In the above Activity, body language confirmed the message being given. However, body language can be very subtle – like a whisper. A look which goes on a fraction too long, the slightest glance at a wristwatch – examples like these can convey feelings we might prefer to keep hidden.

Activity 30

5 mins

A member of your workteam has come to you with a suggestion for improving work methods.

Your words to her are: 'I think that's a very good idea. I'll certainly think very seriously about adopting it.'

Your body language is:

- you avoid meeting her eyes;
- you finger your collar;
- you back away from her while speaking.

What message does that person actually receive from your behaviour?

_____
_____

You might have interpreted the message as: 'I think that's a lousy idea and in no way am I going to use it.'

Did you agree? Our body language can sometimes let us down by conveying a totally different message from the spoken word. When body language contradicts speech, we often pay more attention to what we see than what we hear and respond to the behaviour rather than the words.

> Actions speak louder than words.

Session B

This brings us to another important point about our behaviour. We can deliberately use body language to confirm what we are saying – our behaviour is intentional. However, a great deal of our body language may be unconscious – much of the time we are not aware of the non-verbal signals we are giving to other people. When we are caught in unguarded moments we may well communicate messages we do not intend other people to receive. There's an example of this below.

- John Olumide had been confident that he would be promoted to the post of supervisor in his section. When he was called into the office, he expected his manager to congratulate him. Instead, she told him that she was sorry but she was promoting an older member of the workteam who had more experience. John attempted to hid his disappointment and said: 'That's great! Jenny deserves it.'

However, as he said the words:

- his shoulders slumped;
- the expectant broad smile on his face was replace by one that was fixed;
- he avoided meeting her eyes.

Unintentionally he had conveyed his disappointment through his body language.

> **EXTENSION 2**
> Brush up your body language with *Body Talk: The Skills of Positive Image* by Judi James.

Frequently we can send unintentional behavioural messages. This can present a barrier to good communication – one which we may not even be aware of.

As a manager you need to use body language intentionally and positively to help you in your job.

One problem that often worries newly appointed supervisors is whether they appear sufficiently assertive to their workteam so that they gain their co-operation and respect. Some may overdo assertiveness and show aggressive behaviour; others may lack confidence and show themselves to be rather weak. In the next Activity we have shown some typical behavioural signals which convey this attitude.

Session B

Activity 31

8 mins

For each type of behaviour listed, tick whether you would consider it a sign of aggression, assertiveness or weakness.

	Behaviour		
	Aggressive	Assertive	Weak
Jabbing a finger at someone when giving an instruction	☐	☐	☐
Maintaining frequent eye contact when talking to a member of your workteam	☐	☐	☐
Sitting hunched over your desk and fiddling with your papers when disciplining a member of your workteam	☐	☐	☐
Leaning forward slightly and smiling at an applicant in a selection interview	☐	☐	☐
Drumming your fingers on the desk while explaining a technical detail.	☐	☐	☐

You probably agreed that aggressive behaviour was shown by:

- jabbing a finger;
- drumming your fingers on the desk.

Weak behaviour was shown by:

- sitting hunched over your desk;
- fiddling with papers.

Assertive behaviour was shown by:

- frequent eye contact;
- leaning forward slightly and smiling.

Session B

You need to adopt assertive behaviour. Here are some examples of positive body language, which you can use to show assertiveness in a variety of situations.

- Frequent eye contact

    You can use your eyes to establish contact, develop a rapport and show interest.

- A range of facial expressions

    You should allow your face to support your message. This means displaying a whole range of emotions through the way that you look. An aggressive person will look constantly bad-tempered while a weak person will always look anxious.

- Upright but relaxed posture

    This applies whether standing or sitting. Good posture actually conveys confidence, alertness and interest as well as helping you to breathe and speak more easily.

- Open gestures

    You will find that assertiveness can be conveyed through certain gestures. For example, use a firm handshake when greeting people. If you are using your hands when explaining a point, then use them with the palms upwards to show sincerity and honesty. Crossing your arms in front of your body suggests defensiveness or withdrawal.

    Body language is an essential part of communicating to your workteam. Another form of behaviour that can act as a form of communication to your workteam is the way you carry out your own work. Bad attitudes to work can quickly be communicated to other people and then influence their own behaviour, as in the example below.

- Frank was the supervisor in the order processing section. Despite being a 'tough' supervisor, his workteam had the worst attendance record in the department and an increasing number of errors were found in their orders. Frank blamed his workteam for shoddy work.

    In one exit interview with a clerk who was leaving, it came to light that the team had stopped caring about their work because Frank didn't seem to worry about anything except the number of orders they processed. He took long tea breaks and frequently wandered off to other sections while they were working.

    The team had taken their lead from Frank. He had set them a bad example and they had followed it.

Session B

Setting a good example is part of behavioural communication. Some of the examples we set may be determined or aided by the symbols that surround our jobs. Some front line managers wear different clothes to distinguish them from members of the workteam – uniforms are a common form of behavioural communication. They tell people about authority and status.

Activity 32

5 mins

Try to identify **two** other symbols which surround your own job that convey messages about your authority and status.

_____
_____
_____
_____

You might have thought of more than two. I have chosen some typical status symbols in my list. These are:

- a personalized parking space in the car park;
- a different kind of desk or chair;
- whether you have to clock on for work;
- the canteen in which you eat.

You may not be able to control this kind of behavioural message – it goes with the job – but it is just as well to be aware that it exists!

Now you are ready to think about developing your own behavioural communication skills. In doing this you should:

- think about the impact of your body language on others;
- use behaviour that reinforces your words to ensure the right action.

Session B

Portfolio of evidence C4.1, D1.2

Activity 33

15 mins

This Activity may provide the basis of appropriate evidence for your S/NVQ portfolio. If you are intending to take this course of action, it might be better to write your answers on separate sheets of paper.

Ask your communications partner for an honest commentary on your body language. Does your behaviour indicate aggressiveness, weakness or defensiveness, assertiveness or confidence?

Ask your communications partner to give specific instances rather than generalized comments. If it is possible unobtrusively to have yourself recorded with a video camera, take advantage of the opportunity even though you may find the prospect somewhat daunting.

If you find some behaviour which detracts from the message you want to convey, make a conscious effort to change. If you have time, keep a daily log of your efforts, your feelings about the changed behaviour and the response that you get for a week or so.

This may sound like an enormous effort for little quantifiable result but this kind of 'conversation' with yourself can be very revealing about how you feel about work and your own performance and can be quite helpful in enabling you to address issues which you are usually too busy to allow to the surface.

This session of the workbook has looked at the skills you use as a sender when communicating. The next session will consider the main skill needed by receivers – the ability to listen.

Session B

Self-assessment 2

5 mins

Complete the following sentences with a suitable word or words chosen from this list.

PLANNING   BRIEF   PERMANENT
YOU   RECORD   ACCURATE
INTENTIONAL POSITIVE   BEHAVIOURAL
UNCONSCIOUS METHOD   BODY LANGUAGE

1 Effective communication means being _____, _____ and clear.

2 It is important to think carefully about your written communication because it is projecting an image of _____.

3 Written communication allows more time for _____, but once committed to paper, it is a _____ _____.

4 Eye contact, facial expressions, gestures and posture are often referred to as _____ _____.

5 Setting a good example is a form of _____ communication.

6 Successful communication means selecting the right _____ for the situation.

7 A great deal of body language is _____.

8 A front line manager's use of body language should be _____ and _____.

Answers to these questions can be found on page 78.

8 Summary

- The structure of an organization affects:
    - the structure or systems of communication;
    - the culture;
    - the way communication is managed.

Session B

- Whenever you speak or write, remember the basic principles of communication:
  - accuracy;
  - brevity;
  - clarity;
  - clear communication;
  - complete communication;
  - concise communication;
  - correct communication;
  - courteous communication.

- You should select a method of communication that is suited to any situation bearing in mind:
  - clarity;
  - speed;
  - cost effectiveness;
  - attitude of receiver.

- It is important to remember that every piece of writing is projecting an image of you.

- In order to convey a written message that is understood and acted upon, keep your reader in the forefront of your mind.

- In speaking to others, engage brain before opening mouth.

- In order to convey a spoken message well:
  - prepare;
  - switch on the listener;
  - speak clearly and audibly;
  - use familiar words and phrases;
  - use a tone which reflects the message;
  - ask for playback.

- Behavioural messages can be conveyed through:
  - eye contact;
  - facial expression;
  - gestures;
  - stance and posture.

- Remember that where there is a contradiction between speech and behaviour, actions speak louder than words.

- Develop body language which is:
  - positive;
  - intentional.

Session C The skill of listening

1 Introduction

> There is no bigger respect you can pay colleagues than to hear their point of view.

You have seen that front line managers and team leaders need to be competent as senders in the communication process; they also need to be effective receivers. Information, instructions, advice, questions and requests will come from the workteam, management and other sections and you have a responsibility to listen. Listening is the key to understanding and taking appropriate action. It is also the basis of good relationships at work. You will know yourself that if somebody actually listens to you, the feeling of understanding may help to dissolve a problem. Your colleagues will appreciate the time you take to listen to them.

> **EXTENSION 3**
> If you want to find out more about how to develop your listening skills, you will find some useful information in *Listen Up – Hear What's Really Being Said* by Jim Dugger.

2 The importance of listening

Let's begin by looking at the importance of listening skills and then investigate how we often allow ourselves to be poor listeners. Finally, there are some practical points on how you can improve your own listening skills.

Activity 34 (6 mins)

Why do you think it is necessary to be a good listener in your role? Try to jot down **three** reasons.

_____
_____
_____

Session C

Listening is a vital skill at work. Listening enables you to:

- act on instructions and advice quickly and accurately;
- pick up good ideas from other people;
- discover why members of your workteam hold certain attitudes towards you and their work;
- understand problems and difficulties;
- be more approachable as a leader of your workteam when dealing with complaints, problems etc.

The two-way communication process cannot be effective unless you listen, understand and act. In other words, you cannot do your job properly unless you are prepared to listen carefully.

> Listening is an essential part of the communication process.

You have probably recognized this as good common sense; it is surprising how easy it is for us to lapse into being poor listeners.

3 Barriers to effective listening

One of the basic reasons for poor listening is our own attitude to this activity. We tend to consider it an automatic process. If someone is speaking, because we hear the words, we assume we are listening. This is often not the case. We should never confuse hearing with listening. Hearing is a passive experience. Hearing is expecting our ears to do all the work. Listening involves the mind actually using its existing knowledge to make sense of the new information. It is hearing and interpreting information so that we understand and act correctly.

> Listening is an active process.

When we view listening as a passive experience we fall prey to a number of practices which interfere with our ability to listen.

Session C

Activity 35

6 mins

Think back to an occasion when you were being briefed by your manager or were sitting in a meeting and you were conscious that you were not listening properly.

- What affected your ability to listen?

_____
_____
_____
_____

In your answer, have you blamed the speaker or yourself?

_____

Of course there are some speakers that make it very difficult for their listeners – they are inaudible, muddled or vague. However, most of the fault lies with the listener. For example, as a listener you may:

- become absorbed in noticing distracting features about the speaker rather than concentrating on the substance of the message; for example, you may be distracted by a physical characteristic or a mannerism;
- allow distractions in your environment to disturb your concentration too easily; this may be someone walking past, the ringing of a telephone or the behaviour of other people in the room;
- fail to look at the speaker so that you miss the behavioural signals which help you to understand the message;
- 'switch off' deliberately because you have taken offence at the tone of the speaker or reacted emotionally to a phrase he or she has used;
- allow the fact that you don't like the speaker to block your concentration;
- try to do two things at once such as trying to write a memo at the same time as listening to an instruction or simply continue thinking about something else which seems more important or urgent at the time.

We can summarize these various faults by saying that listeners can often be distracted from the substance of the message by:

- the speaker;
- their environment;
- their own feelings and attitudes.

Once you recognize these are common faults to which we all succumb and realize that you may also behave in this way, you are half-way to improving your listening skills.

Session C

Almost everybody working at the moment feels him- or herself to be under a lot of pressure with more to do in the course of the day than can actually be achieved. If that is how you are feeling, listening becomes increasingly difficult because it requires you to focus your attention on one thing when the chances are that your mind is easily distracted on to half a dozen other things which you feel you should be dealing with at the same time.

Yet the ability to listen and to give what you are hearing your whole attention is a valuable management skill.

Major innovations in any organization, such as the decision to change the product or service offered or to relocate, tend to come from above. Actually making things work, however, often results from a hundred small innovations and they usually come from below. As a front line manager you are in touch (if you're listening!) with that source of good ideas and practical solutions from which more senior managers tend to be distanced. You are the channel for relaying the ideas and you are uniquely well-placed to do this.

Being in the habit of listening thoughtfully also helps you to anticipate problems. Charles Northcote Parkinson said that it is a sign of management failure when a deputation comes to complain. The hard fact is that you should have been listening and you should have known sooner. A grievance, like a mutiny at sea, does not spring up without any warning. There will have been oblique comments and half hints which a tuned-in manager will have picked up and tried to respond to.

4 Characteristics of good listeners

There are some practical steps you can take to improve your own listening skills. These all lie within your control. The next Activity encourages you to identify some of the characteristics of good listeners from your own observation or experience.

Activity 36

5 mins

Good listeners concentrate on the substance of the message. Write down **three** other things that good listeners do.

_____

_____

_____

Session C

Here is a list of things that good listeners tend to do.

- Keep your eyes focused on the speaker. This enables you to interpret the body language as well as listen to the words.
- Meet the sender's eye as often as possible.
- Let the sender make his or her points. Don't interrupt.
- Use simple phrases, words or noises that show that you are giving the words your attention while not interrupting the speaker. Some examples are 'I see', 'OK', 'Umm'.
- Show attention by body language and facial expression: nodding, looking at the speaker, not fidgeting or looking round the room. Sitting quietly and still, leaning slightly forwards is a clear indication that you are ready to listen. Facial expression can show doubt, pleasure, anxiety, anger – make sure you are aware of what others may see in your face.
- Concentrate on key phrases, stressed words. By doing this it's possible to extract the essential information from surrounding detail.
- Write down brief notes. This ensures that you have got key facts correct, particularly if the message is long, complex or involves detailed instructions.
- Ask questions. Questions allow the speaker to clear up misunderstandings and to find out any additional information they need.
- Offer feedback. This enables you to show that you have understood the message correctly and are prepared to act.

Activity 37

Portfolio of evidence C4.1, D1.1

10 mins

This Activity may provide the basis of appropriate evidence for your S/NVQ portfolio. If you are intending to take this course of action, it might be better to write your answers on separate sheets of paper.

Next time you have to listen to somebody for any length of time (e.g. at a meeting or presentation) use the features of a good listener listed above as a checklist and make a conscious effort to demonstrate them all.

Session C

Afterwards, briefly assess how you measured up to each of the features and how much you got out of the discussion in terms of:

- the completeness, accuracy and relevance of the information you obtained;
- the responsiveness of the speaker towards you.

_____
_____
_____
_____
_____
_____
_____
_____
_____

This may sound rather calculating and artificial, especially when you are not going to achieve a spectacular improvement overnight. But listening **is** just a skill like any other and practising it until it becomes second nature will deliver results.

If you can use these simple techniques yourself, you will be a more effective listener in face-to-face situations. Listening is a much easier activity when sender and receiver can see one another. This is because you use body language as a listener just as much as you do as a speaker.

Telephone conversations are more difficult because there is no body language to help you.

Activity 38

5 mins

What techniques can you use in your telephone conversation to demonstrate that you are listening actively to the other person? Jot down **one** or **two** ideas.

_____
_____

Session C

You could:

- use 'Yes', 'I see', 'uh hmm' when the sender is giving detailed information and a longer reply might distract them;
- ask follow-up questions on the information given, which show that you have received and understood the message;
- repeat key facts: times, dates, numbers.

As you can see, on the telephone your other communication skills must compensate for the absence of body language.

Activity 39

15 mins

Arrange a listening session with your communications partner. Each of you should take it in turns to speak for two minutes, about a mutually agreed topic, without interruption from the other. The listener must try to remember as much as possible of what has been said. When the speaker has finished speaking, the listener should summarize what has been said. The speaker should make corrections or help you to fill gaps.

What did you notice when doing this exercise?

_____
_____
_____
_____
_____

You may have realized that two minutes is actually a very long time – both to speak and to listen. Most people find it hard to remember what the other person said. This could be because it was hard to concentrate, or because you weren't really interested, or because for some reason you didn't want to hear the words which were being said, for example if the topic was a difficult or painful one or about something with which you violently disagree. It is a good idea to repeat this exercise every now and again. You will get better with practice, and you will also become aware of what stops you from listening.

You might also like to test your concentration by listening to a news bulletin on the radio and then recalling all the news items in the right order. You will need to tape the bulletin as well to check whether you were correct.

Session C

One of the benefits of being a good listener is that it tends to improve other people's communication skills. Public speakers will tell you that an attentive, interested audience can really help them to improve their own delivery: the rapport has been established. The same is true at work. If you can show yourself to be a good listener, you will often help other people to speak more clearly and accurately. Good communication will almost inevitably improve relationships between people as well, so listening is one of the first steps to ensuring good working relationships.

5 Listening to behaviour

So far, we have used the word 'listening' as a process involving the ears and the brain. A good dictionary would also explain listening as 'paying attention to'. We are going to use the word in this context in this last section. Team leaders need to pay attention to behavioural messages from their workteam.

Marked changes in behaviour, particularly a fall in performance, are often signs that someone has a problem. We need to be able to spot these signals as soon as possible and respond to them.

Imagine, for example, that a pleasant, punctual, hardworking machinist changes overnight – she arrives late on two consecutive days, is surly and becomes increasingly careless in her work. If you are 'listening' to her behaviour it should tell you that something is wrong and that, as the supervisor, you must deal with this problem.

Other behavioural symptoms that team leaders need to note are aggressiveness or defensiveness in members of their workteam. Where these occur, the underlying cause could be that the person feels threatened or under some kind of stress. Too often we can dismiss this type of behaviour as someone 'going through a rough patch' or 'in one of their moods' and pay very little attention to it. Paying heed to behavioural communication is the first step to solving the problem. Failing to take notice of these signals will only allow the situation to get worse. It is therefore important that you pay attention to behaviour as well as words.

Let's now look at these ideas in a practical situation in the following incident.

Session C

Activity 40

5 mins

- Harry Wrath is a skilled lathe operator. About six months ago the company for which he then worked made half the workforce redundant to new technology. Harry was one of those to go. Fortunately he got a new job quickly and settled in well – he enjoyed working for his new firm.

    After four months he and others were informed by their supervisor that the firm was to introduce computer-assisted machines which were needed for the firm to remain competitive. The supervisor made it clear that Harry and the others would not lose their jobs. Privately, the supervisor considered it would benefit them in terms of increased pay and improved working conditions.

    Harry's attitude to his work began to deteriorate. His supervisor found him rude and difficult to handle. Harry tried to persuade the union branch to oppose the introduction of the new technology. When this wasn't accepted Harry became even more difficult. He became argumentative and unpleasant.

What do you think was the cause of the change in Harry's behaviour?

_____

_____

If you were Harry's supervisor would you:

- Ignore his behaviour? ☐
- Tell him to pull himself together? ☐
- Talk to him about his opposition? ☐
- Report him to your manager? ☐

Harry lost his last job when new technology was introduced and this is obviously still on his mind. He is probably very worried that the same thing may happen again. In addition, many people find change very difficult to handle – and this may have felt like one change too many, after the successful job change.

The most useful action you can take is talk to him about his opposition to the change. In reality this means giving him the chance to talk. You must listen to him to find out fully why his opposition is so strong and then use your own knowledge about the details of the new technology to be introduced to show him how it will help him, rather than deprive him of his job. Only a full and frank exchange of information is likely to help his behaviour return to normal. Your honesty and willingness to listen will also help to cement your own relationship with Harry.

One way to develop your ability to 'listen to behaviour' and to interpret other people's body language is to watch a silent film such as one starring Charlie Chaplin or Laurel and Hardy; alternatively, you could watch television with

Session C

the sound turned right down or watch programmes which are intended for deaf people. When people communicate in sign language, they use their whole bodies and a great deal of facial expression. Trying to work out what people mean without the benefit of words will sharpen your powers of observation very quickly.

Effective communication is not always easy but when the process is successful it does make the work of a supervisor more productive and less frustrating. It also goes a long way towards ensuring good working relationships which in turn is likely to have a beneficial effect on the work being done.

Self-assessment 3

5 mins

Complete the following sentences with a suitable word or words selected from the list below.

SPEAKER	UNDERSTAND	DEMONSTRATE
LISTENER	ACT	ENVIRONMENT
BEHAVIOUR	DEFENSIVENESS	SUBSTANCE
EYES	ACTIVE	

1 The two-way communication process requires that you listen, _____ and _____.

2 Poor listening is the fault of the _____.

3 Good listeners _____ they are listening.

4 You should pay attention to _____ as well as listening to words when communicating with your workteam.

5 Listeners can be distracted from the _____ of the message by the speaker, their _____ or their own feelings and attitudes.

6 Listening is an _____ process.

7 Good listeners focus their _____ on the _____.

8 Behavioural symptoms that indicate that a member of your workteam may be under pressure are aggressiveness and _____.

Answers to these questions can be found on pages 78–9.

Session C

6 Summary

- Listening is an essential part of the communication process.

- Hearing is not the same as listening.

- You can't help hearing: listening needs thinking about.

- Effective listening helps to improve working relationships.

- Most listening faults are because the listener becomes distracted by:
  - the speaker;
  - their environment;
  - their own attitudes and feelings.

- The characteristics of good listeners are that they:
  - focus their eyes on the speaker;
  - let the sender make his or her points;
  - demonstrate they are listening;
  - concentrate on key phrases and stressed words;
  - write down brief notes;
  - ask questions;
  - offer feedback.

- A good supervisor also pays attention to behaviour as well as words, particularly changes in behaviour.

Performance checks

1 Quick quiz

Jot down answers to the following questions on *Communication in Management*.

Question 1   How would you define 'communication'?

Question 2   Why is it so important to communicate?

Question 3   Draw or explain a model of the communication process.

Question 4   What are the main barriers to communication?

Question 5   Why is feedback so important?

Performance checks

Question 6 Describe the **three** main ways in which communication flows.

Question 7 Define and describe the ABC of good communication.

Question 8 When deciding between written and spoken communication what factors should you consider?

Question 9 Why is it important to pay attention to body language?

Question 10 List **four** examples of positive, assertive body language.

Question 11 Why is listening, especially at work, such a vital skill?

Performance checks

Question 12   Why do people often fail to listen?

Question 13   List at least **six** things you can do to show that you are really listening.

Question 14   How can it be helpful to 'listen' or pay attention to changes in behaviour?

Question 15   List **three** benefits of effective communication.

Answers to these questions can be found on pages 79–81.

Performance checks

2 Workbook assessment

60 mins

Read the following case incident, and then deal with the questions that follow. Write your answers on a separate sheet of paper.

■ The past year had been a little unsettled at Kay's Castings. During the year a number of rumours had arisen about the company's future. One rumour hinted at an expansion of the labour force, only to be followed shortly after by another about redundancy. The latest rumour, which arose from the current wage negotiations, suggested that Kay's was to be taken over by a larger group of companies. This rumour was denied by Kay's management as quite unfounded.

For several weeks the personnel office had been preparing for a visit by a group of City stockbrokers. These visits were quite common and helped the 'City' to keep in touch with companies in whose shares they were dealing.

There was nothing sinister in the visit, but rumours soon began to get around. On the day of the visit Kay's directors were out in force – each of them showed their group of visitors round the factory.

Paul Dunn was a long-serving and loyal member of the workforce – he was also one of the trade union shop stewards. He normally acted very sensibly and calmly, but on the day of the visit he acted very aggressively. Although he had been informed about the purpose of the visit, he stormed into his manager's office. 'What's really going on with this visit? I asked a couple of them what they are here for and couldn't get any sense out of them!'

Lewis Stewart, the manager, was already having an anxious time keeping production going whilst at the same time attempting to impress his directors and visitors. His reply was quite short, 'Look Paul, you were told six weeks ago what the visit was for. These people can make or break a company like ours. The last thing they want to see is your machine idle – so why not get back to your job and leave me to get on with mine'.

Paul returned to his machine angry and worried. When tea break came Paul took the opportunity to work off his anger at Lewis and the visitors by grumbling to his mates. After a while the whole section was angry and worried. The result was that whenever the opportunity arose, they stood around and angrily talked with each other. A lot of this took place around the doors of the washroom and had also begun to interfere with the access to Lewis Stewart's office.

---

1 List **two** likely causes of the rumours.

2 Why does Paul Dunn deserve better treatment from his manager than he actually received?

3 Show how our four-point planning approach what, who, how, why would have improved Lewis Stewart's communication with Paul Dunn.

4 What was the feedback that Lewis Stewart appeared to ignore?

Performance checks

3 Work-based assignment

Portfolio of evidence C4.1, D1.1, D1.2

60 mins

The time guide for this assignment gives you an approximate idea of how long it is likely to take you to write up your findings. You will find you need to spend some additional time gathering information, perhaps talking to colleagues and thinking about the assignment. The result of your efforts should be presented on separate sheets of paper.

Your written response to this assignment should form useful evidence for your S/NVQ portfolio. The assignment is designed to help you demonstrate your Personal Competence in:

- relating to others;
- communicating.

What you have to do

Recall two communication situations in which you have been involved. You may see yourself as principally the receiver or the transmitter of the message. You should choose one example of an effective communication and one example where communication went wrong.

Analyse each situation using our communication model. It is repeated here to remind you.

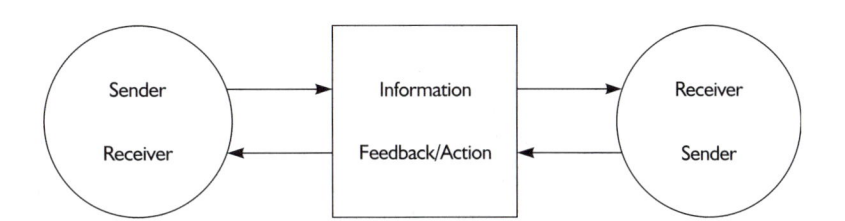

```
     Sender    →   Information   →    Receiver
                                      
     Receiver  ←   Feedback/Action ←  Sender
```

In your analysis you should describe each stage and why one communication was effective and why the other failed.

What were the lessons you learned from these two situations and how successful have you been in changing your communication technique as a result?

What was the effect of the way you communicated in each of these situations on your relationship with the other people involved?

Reflect and review

1 Reflect and review

Now that you have completed your work on *Communication in Management*, let us review our workbook objectives.

At the end of this workbook you should be better able to:

- identify the benefits to you of being a good communicator.

Communication is essential to good management, therefore understanding what is involved in the communication process and using that process more effectively will enable you to be a better leader, planner, organizer and co-ordinator.

- **How can I carry out an audit of present communication so that it will be possible to measure improvements?**

  _____

  _____

- **What tangible benefits are likely to result from improved communications at work?**

  _____

  _____

The second objective was that you should be better able to:

- design your communications to achieve the results you want.

After learning about the communication process and some of the techniques of writing, speaking and behaving, you should be able to plan your communication to convey information accurately, briefly and clearly to your workteam, and secure feedback from them so that you can be certain they will act on the information in the correct way.

- **Can I draw up a set of guidelines for planning written communications?**

  _____

  _____

Reflect and review

- **How can I ensure that I choose the method of communication which will best suit my purpose?**

  _____

  _____

The third objective was that you should be better able to:

■ communicate more effectively in speech, writing and behaviour.

You can use the ABC and five Cs of communication as a simple guide for all your communication. If you adopt the suggestions made in the sections on writing, speaking and behaving and carry out your Action plan, you will find that your own communication will continue to improve.

- **How can I ensure that my communications have been effective/ successful?**

  _____

  _____

- **What can I do to monitor my body language so that it reinforces the message I want to communicate?**

  _____

  _____

The last objective was that you should be better able to:

■ listen effectively.

Now you are aware of how and why we tend to be poor listeners, you can adopt a more positive and active approach to listening to words and behaviour so that you can provide accurate person and action feedback to others.

- **How can I demonstrate to my team that I want to listen to what they have to say?**

  _____

  _____

- **How can I use feedback to monitor the quality/effectiveness of my listening?**

  _____

  _____

Reflect and review

2 Action plan

Use this plan to further develop for yourself a course of action you want to take. Make a note in the left-hand column of the issues or problems you want to tackle, and then decide what you intend to do, and make a note in Column 2.

The resources you need might include time, materials, information or money. You may need to negotiate for some of them, but they could be something easily acquired, like half an hour of somebody's time, or a chapter of a book. Put whatever you need in Column 3. No plan means anything without a timescale, so put a realistic target completion date in Column 4.

Finally, describe the outcome you want to achieve as a result of this plan, whether it is for your own benefit or advancement, or a more efficient way of doing things.

Desired outcomes					Actual outcomes
	1 Issues	2 Action	3 Resources	4 Target completion	

Reflect and review

3 Extensions

Extension 1

Video   *Frontliners*
Publisher   BBC Training Videos

This series of three videos shows you communication where it should be, in the context of achieving a business result. *You and Your Workforce* focuses on, among other things, the importance of sharing information and of listening. *You and Your Organization* includes the importance of being genuine and coming across as enthusiastic and illustrates how you can earn respect by the way you communicate within and outside the workteam.

Extension 2

Book   *Body Talk: The Skills of Positive Image*
Author   Judi James
Edition   1995
Publisher   Industrial Society

A practical and more in-depth consideration of body language than is possible within the scope of this workbook.

Extension 3

Book   *Listen Up – Hear What's Really Being Said*
Author   Jim Dugger
Edition   1995
Publisher   American Media Publishing

This book covers a lot of relevant and useful topics, including Chapter 4 which contains some useful advice on listening.

These Extensions can be taken up via your NEBS Management Centre. They will either have them or will arrange that you have access to them. However, it may be more convenient to check out the materials with your personnel or training people at work – they may well give you access. There are other good reasons for approaching your own people; for example, they will become aware of your interest and you can involve them in your development.

4 Answers to self-assessment questions

Self-assessment 1 on page 28

1 a The communication model has three key features; these are: **INFORMATION**, people and **ACTION**.
    b Feedback can come from action and from **PEOPLE**.
    c Action can involve a change of **MIND** as well as a change of behaviour.
    d Our four-point planning method asks what, why, **WHO** and **HOW**.

Reflect and review

   e   Some barriers to communication include **FEELINGS, LANGUAGE, CULTURE** and environment.
   f   **FEEDBACK** is essential to the communication process.
   g   Our **EXPERIENCE** and **ATTITUDES** affect the way we communicate.
   h   All communication needs to be **PLANNED**.

2 You can make sure that the receiver of a written communication has understood by:

   - asking specific questions;
   - stating the kind of response you want;
   - stating the action you want in the last sentence.

3 The amount of time you spend planning communications will be affected by:

   - your knowledge and experience;
   - the other person's knowledge and experience;
   - the seriousness of failing to communicate effectively;
   - how well you know and get on with the other person;
   - the complexity of the communication which needs to be communicated.

Self-assessment 2 on page 53

1 Effective communication means being **ACCURATE, BRIEF** and clear.

2 It is important to think carefully about your written communication because it is projecting an image of **YOU**.

3 Written communication allows more time for **PLANNING**, but once committed to paper, it is a **PERMANENT RECORD**.

4 Eye contact, facial expressions, gestures and posture are often referred to as **BODY LANGUAGE**.

5 Setting a good example is a form of **BEHAVIOURAL** communication.

6 Successful communication means selecting the right **METHOD** for the situation.

7 A great deal of body language is **UNCONSCIOUS**.

8 A front line manager's use of body language should be **INTENTIONAL** and **POSITIVE**.

Self-assessment 3 on page 64

1 The two-way communication process requires that you listen, **understand** and **act**.

2 Poor listening is the fault of the **LISTENER**.

3 Good listeners **DEMONSTRATE** they are listening.

Reflect and review

4   You should pay attention to **BEHAVIOUR** as well as listen to words when communicating with your workteam.

5   Listeners can be distracted from the **SUBSTANCE** of the message by the speaker, their **ENVIRONMENT** or their own feelings and attitudes.

6   Listening is an **ACTIVE** process.

7   Good listeners focus their **EYES** on the **SPEAKER**.

8   Behavioural symptoms that indicate that a member of your workteam is under pressure are aggressiveness and **DEFENSIVENESS**.

5 Answers to the quick quiz

Answer 1   Communication can be defined as the transfer of information between two or more people, usually resulting in action. It is always a two-way process.

Answer 2   Communication is important to to ensure that tasks are carried out in the right way. You need to be able to communicate at work in order to instruct, inform, persuade, encourage, suggest, consult and negotiate. Good communication is also the basis for good relationships. So communication between people at all levels at work is crucial.

Answer 3   Any model of communication should include a sender, a receiver, the information to be sent and received and the result (feedback or action) arising from the communication. The model should indicate the circular or two-way nature of communication – true communication never happens in isolation. It may also indicate the organization and/or the culture which influence the communication.

Answer 4   The main barriers to communication are

- noise – which can make it difficult to hear or concentrate;
- the environment – the layout of offices may make it hard to concentrate or listen to what people are saying;
- language – words can be misinterpreted or misunderstood, especially if jargon or imprecise language ('sort of', 'ummm', 'things') are used;
- feelings – if we are upset about something or have negative feelings about someone, we may not hear what they are saying, or we may not be able to concentrate on what is being said;
- authority relationships – if information has to go through certain channels to reach the people who need to receive it, it may be transformed, misinterpreted or delayed;
- culture – if people are unfamiliar with the prevailing culture in the organization, they may observe a different set of communication 'rules'. It may be alright to communicate verbally in a friendly and informal way in one organization, while the need for formal written records may dominate the way communication is carried out elsewhere.

Reflect and review

Answer 5 Feedback is essential for us to know that our message has been received and understood. The best form of feedback is action, so that you can be sure that your message has been interpreted correctly.

Answer 6 Communication normally flows in three directions:

- downwards from management to staff, instructing workers, explaining jobs, providing performance feedback and telling new employees what is expected;
- upwards from staff to management, providing feedback about how workers feel about their work, what problems they encounter, and what changes may be needed;
- horizontally between workers, to co-ordinate tasks, share information, solve problems and provide support.

Answer 7 The ABC of good communication refers to the need for:

- accuracy – information must be correct and up to date;
- brevity – information should be relevant, to the point and expressed concisely;
- clarity – information must be clear so that the meaning cannot be misunderstood.

Answer 8 The decision to write or speak should be taken after considering these factors:

- clarity – how will the information be conveyed most clearly and accurately?
- speed – how quickly must the other person receive and act on the message?
- cost effectiveness – which method will achieve the necessary result for the least cost?
- attitude of receivers – which method will be most acceptable to the receivers? (This may depend partly on the organizational culture.)

Answer 9 Body language is an important part of communication because 'actions speak louder than words'. We can be betrayed by our body language if we don't really mean what we say; equally, our body language can reinforce our message if we are conscious of it.

Answer 10 Using assertive and positive body language will be to your advantage, and includes:

- frequent eye contact;
- range of facial expressions;
- an upright but relaxed posture;
- open gestures (such as a firm handshake, a straight gaze).

Answer 11 Listening is an important skill which helps you to:

- act on instructions and advice;
- pick up good ideas;
- find out what members of your workteam think;
- understand problems and difficulties;
- be more approachable as a leader.

Reflect and review

Answer 12 People may fail to listen for one of the following reasons:

- they notice distracting things about the speaker (such as fidgeting, or other physical characteristics);
- they are distracted by something or someone in the environment;
- they fail to look at the speaker, so missing important behavioural clues;
- they deliberately switch off because of an emotional reaction to something the speaker has said or the way she or he has said it;
- they don't like the speaker and so don't bother to hear what he or she is saying;
- they try to do two (or more) things at once, perhaps writing a memo at the same time as attempting to listen to instructions.

Answer 13 Good listeners:

- keep their eyes focused on the speaker;
- meet the sender's eyes as often as possible;
- don't interrupt;
- indicate that they are listening by saying things like 'I see', 'uh hmm', 'OK';
- indicate attentiveness through body language and facial expression;
- concentrate on key phrases and stressed words;
- write brief notes;
- ask questions;
- offer feedback.

Answer 14 Paying attention to changes in behaviour can provide vital clues to problems someone may be experiencing. It is then possible to respond to the problem quickly, or at least to follow up your hunch that something may be wrong.

Answer 15 Effective communication has many benefits including:

- ensuring good working relationships;
- reducing frustration;
- enhancing the work which is being done;
- increasing productivity.

Reflect and review

6 Certificate

Completion of this certificate by an authorized person shows that you have worked through all the parts of this workbook and satisfactorily completed the assessments. The certificate provides a record of what you have done that may be used for exemptions or as evidence of prior learning against other nationally certificated qualifications.

Pergamon Open Learning and NEBS Management are always keen to refine and improve their products. One of the key sources of information to help this process are people who have just used the product. If you have any information or views, good or bad, please pass these on.

NEBS MANAGEMENT DEVELOPMENT
SUPER SERIES
THIRD EDITION

Communication in Management

....

has satisfactorily completed this workbook

Name of signatory ....

Position ....

Signature ....

Date ....

Official stamp

SUPER SERIES

SUPER SERIES 3
0-7506-3362-X   Full Set of Workbooks, User Guide and Support Guide

A. Managing Activities
0-7506-3295-X	1. Planning and Controlling Work
0-7506-3296-8	2. Understanding Quality
0-7506-3297-6	3. Achieving Quality
0-7506-3298-4	4. Caring for the Customer
0-7506-3299-2	5. Marketing and Selling
0-7506-3300-X	6. Managing a Safe Environment
0-7506-3301-8	7. Managing Lawfully - Health, Safety and Environment
0-7506-37064	8. Preventing Accidents
0-7506-3302-6	9. Leading Change
0-7506-4091-X	10. Auditing Quality

B. Managing Resources
0-7506-3303-4	1. Controlling Physical Resources
0-7506-3304-2	2. Improving Efficiency
0-7506-3305-0	3. Understanding Finance
0-7506-3306-9	4. Working with Budgets
0-7506-3307-7	5. Controlling Costs
0-7506-3308-5	6. Making a Financial Case
0-7506-4092-8	7. Managing Energy Efficiency

C. Managing People
0-7506-3309-3	1. How Organisations Work
0-7506-3310-7	2. Managing with Authority
0-7506-3311-5	3. Leading Your Team
0-7506-3312-3	4. Delegating Effectively
0-7506-3313-1	5. Working in Teams
0-7506-3314-X	6. Motivating People
0-7506-3315-8	7. Securing the Right People
0-7506-3316-6	8. Appraising Performance
0-7506-3317-4	9. Planning Training and Development
0-75063318-2	10. Delivering Training
0-7506-3320-4	11. Managing Lawfully - People and Employment
0-7506-3321-2	12. Commitment to Equality
0-7506-3322-0	13. Becoming More Effective
0-7506-3323-9	14. Managing Tough Times
0-7506-3324-7	15. Managing Time

D. Managing Information
0-7506-3325-5	1. Collecting Information
0-7506-3326-3	2. Storing and Retrieving Information
0-7506-3327-1	3. Information in Management
0-7506-3328-X	4. Communication in Management
0-7506-3329-8	5. Listening and Speaking
0-7506-3330-1	6. Communicating in Groups
0-7506-3331-X	7. Writing Effectively
0-7506-3332-8	8. Project and Report Writing
0-7506-3333-6	9. Making and Taking Decisions
0-7506-3334-4	10. Solving Problems

SUPER SERIES 3 USER GUIDE + SUPPORT GUIDE
0-7506-37056	1. User Guide
0-7506-37048	2. Support Guide

SUPER SERIES 3 CASSETTE TITLES
0-7506-3707-2	1. Complete Cassette Pack
0-7506-3711-0	2. Reaching Decisions
0-7506-3712-9	3. Making a Financial Case
0-7506-3710-2	4. Customers Count
0-7506-3709-9	5. Being the Best
0-7506-3708-0	6. Working Together

To Order - phone us direct for prices and availability details
(please quote ISBNs when ordering)
College orders: 01865 314333 • Account holders: 01865 314301
Individual purchases: 01865 314627 (please have credit card details ready)

We Need Your Views

We really need your views in order to make the Super Series 3 (SS3) an even better learning tool for you. Please take time out to complete and return this questionnaire to Trudi Righton, Pergamon Open Learning, Linacre House, Jordan Hill, Oxford, OX2 8DP.

Name: ....

Address: ....

....

Title of workbook: ....

If applicable, please state which qualification you are studying for. If not, please describe what study you are undertaking, and with which organisation or college:

....

Please grade the following out of 10 (10 being extremely good, 0 being extremely poor):

Content   ....   Appropriateness to your position   ....

Readability   ....   Qualification coverage   ....

What did you particularly like about this workbook?
....
....
....

Are there any features you disliked about this workbook? Please identify them.
....
....
....

Are there any errors we have missed? If so, please state page number: ....

How are you using the material? For example, as an open learning course, as a reference resource, as a training resource etc.
....

How did you hear about Super Series 3?:

Word of mouth: ☐   Through my tutor/trainer: ☐   Mailshot: ☐

Other (please give details):...
....

Many thanks for your help in returning this form.